Hebridean Hospitality
(An Alternative Guide to The Outer Hebrides)

By Harry Bentley & Chris Duoba

Edited by Leo Turner

Copyright © 2023 Harry Bentley / Chris Duoba / Leo Turner

All rights reserved.

Contents

Introduction/The Scary Hikers are born	Page 5
Day 1 Manchester to Oban	Page 7
Map of The Outer Hebrides	Page 11
Day 2 Oban to Barra	Page 12
Day 3 Castlebay to Eriskay	Page 14
Day 4 Eriskay to Benbecula	Page 18
Day 5 Benbecula to Willie's House	Page 22
Day 6 Benbecula to Lochmaddy	Page 23
Day 7 Leverburgh to Tarbert	Page 29
Day 8 Tarbert	Page 31
Day 9 Tarbert to Stornoway	Page 32
Day 10 The Road to Stornaway	Page 34
Day 11 Stornaway	Page 36
Day 12 Stornaway	Page 38
Day 13 Stornoway & The Butt of Lewis	Page 41
Day 14 Stornaway	Page 43
Day 15 Stornoway to Mangersta	Page 44
Day 16 Eagle's Nest	Page 48
Day 17 Eagle's Nest to Stornaway	Page 50
Day 18 Stornaway to A&E	Page 52
Day 19 Stornaway	Page 54
Day 20 Stornoway	Page 56
Day 21 Stornaway	Page 57
Day 22 Stornaway to Skye	Page 59
Day 23 Dunvegan, Skye	Page 61
Day 24 Skye to Manchester	Page 62
Photos & Maps (in order of heading North)	P64-88
Acknowledgements	Page 89
Contents of Chris's Rucksack	Page 90

INTRODUCTION

Chris Duoba and Harry Bentley have known each other for the best part of twenty years living as neighbours in North Manchester. Chris, being a barber, also used to cut Harry's hair at "The Barbers" in Blackley (Manchester) which was also a while ago now as both Harry and Chris no longer have a single hair between them on both their heads. Both have made up for that though, proudly growing formidable grey beards that have become their trademark and despite their geniality and being the two most approachable people in the world, due to their appearance, have been dubbed the 'Scary Hikers'.

61 year old Chris was a Barber by trade for over 45 years, eventually running his own business before 'retiring' during a Covid lockdown period in 2020 to take care of unfinished business regarding some ambitious physical challenges he still wanted to tackle in his life. Chris is the survivor of a horrific car crash in his late teens that left him with brain and physical injuries that doctors felt would prevent him holding down a job ever again and would limit him physically. Chris went on to own the business he worked in, marry and have four fantastic children and complete several Ironman triathlons and ultra-events that would challenge the fittest of individuals.

77 year old Harry Bentley had ambitions to be a frogman for the Police force back when he was a young man but found himself too small to join the force in 1960 at five foot seven inches. Harry's working career has been varied, ranging from managing and eventually buying his own bakery to working for British Vita with the kind of dangerous chemicals that were later banned. After a spell doing two jobs and running a taxi cab at weekends, Harry saw that running a cab full time was to be the future. Married with two grown up lads that he is super proud of, Harry is an avid and very experienced walker. Like Chris, Harry suffered an accident which left him with an ankle problem that he has ploughed on with and escapes the pressures of life by seeing the beauty of the places he visits. His favourite phrase? 'Once up there in the mountains everyone is a millionaire'

Together, after a chance conversation, they embarked on a 24-day adventure, with just the backpacks on their backs, to one of Britain's most beautiful and remote destinations, The Outer Hebrides. This is their story of the hospitality they received on the islands, taken from Harry's diary across those 24 days.

THE 'SCARY HIKERS' ARE BORN

As next-door neighbours, Chris and Harry had many conversations over the garden fence but none more significant than in June 2021 when Harry told Chris about the 'Pennine Way', a walking trail of over 250 Miles from Derbyshire to Scotland. After some careful briefings from Harry and a short trial run in shocking weather with friend Nathaniel's son, Kane, Chris in typical fashion took off solo in August 2021 to find out for himself what it was all about. He tackled all 256+ miles in just under a month, wild camping, grabbing a bed where he could or seeking refuge in a bothy as he encountered a multitude of life experiences and met some wonderful people. We say 256 miles but Chris actually did more than 300 miles with one or two unintentional detours off the trail.

Another chance conversation between the two of them in November 2021 led to talk of the Outer Hebrides. Harry had always been a keen walker and had said of himself "I might not win any races but I'd certainly outlast many younger people for stamina'. In that first chat about the Outer Hebrides, Harry told Chris that he had just seen Ben Fogle on BBC TV revisiting Taransay, an uninhabited island in the Outer Hebrides, where Ben had his first break as a TV presenter. Fogle had presented the programme 'Castaway' in 2000 where contestants had been left on the Island to fend for themselves for one year in 2000. In the latest TV series that Harry had been watching, Fogle was back in the Outer Hebrides 20 years later and had visited one of the most spectacular Bothies in the world, called 'Eagles Nest' at Mangersta on the Isle of Lewis. A Bothy is a basic shelter usually left unlocked and available for anyone to use free of charge. In this case 'Eagles Nest' bothy was built into a cliff face and was so spectacular and popular with people visiting the islands, it had to be booked in advance. The description Harry gave of the place built into the cliffs made it sound much more suited to a 'Lord of the Rings' film. He had Chris's attention immediately. Harry tried to describe to Chris the kind of place the Outer Hebrides was and summed it up by telling him that he'd heard that The Outer Hebrides can only be compared with two other places. Outer Mongolia and Outer Space" Chris's response? "When are we going?" Harry said that programme and the way it was presented by Ben Fogle, had surprisingly got him emotional. He said that the whole thing had reduced him to tears at times and that he just felt he had to go there and see these islands firsthand and stay a night in the Bothy at 'Eagles Nest'. It is amazing how someone can form such a bond with a place before they have actually visited. As it turns out, that gut instinct that Harry had about the islands was 100% correct and more. As they prepared for the trip both Chris and Harry were giddy with excitement. 'The Eagles Nest' particularly had become a Holy grail for them that they both must experience. As launch day approached, they described the feeling as much like the guy in the film 'Close Encounters of The Third Kind when Richard Dreyfuss' character didn't know why but he was obsessed about a mountain that he had to get to. Equally Chris and Harry felt they had to go to Eagles Nest and it was now becoming an obsession.

Both lads know full well the strength of the human mind and that some of the challenges they might face would be more mental than just physical and one of their reasons for really wanting to do this was to show people that as low as you might feel in your life, something inspirational and memorable might be just around the corner. Chris particularly has struggled with his mental health since his accident in 1980 and openly talks about being close to suicide not long after but now wants to continue to show his real zest for life and potentially convince others in the same situation that there is much to look forward to. The following account of their journey and experiences are based on the daily diary entries of Harry while on their Hebridean adventure and include mention of some of the wonderful Hebridean people that they met along the way that made this adventure such a wonderful experience.

Day 1 – Manchester to Oban - Saturday 7th May 2022

Photo: Piccadilly Setting Off

Long-time friend and editor of this booklet, Leo Turner, waved the intrepid duo off from Piccadilly Station in central Manchester at 7.30am on Saturday 7th May 2022. It had been a crazy two years living through Covid, just as the rest of the world had, dealing with the risks and rules and regulations put in place by the Government. To be free to get a train and start their travels, felt like being set free literally and it was exciting.

Leo said his goodbyes to the lads and spoke later of real concern about what the lads were taking on. This was the Outer Hebrides for Pete's sake. Not unknown for its challenging weather at times and both of the lads were carrying back packs that felt as heavy as a small car. Leo helped them on with the packs and was amazed that they could make it to the platform for the train never mind go trekking on the formidable Hebridean Islands. The packs actually weighed 30kg! Four stone and ten pounds and over thirty kilos in new money. (If you'd like to know what the contents were, we have listed them at the end of the booklet). Initially, the lads started off with the plan that they would head for Fort William and then travel to the Isle of Skye in southwest Scotland and then they would get the ferry over to the port of

Tarbert on the Isle of Lewis. They both desperately wanted to make the most of this experience, so they re-thought the plan a fortnight or so before they left. Instead of heading straight for Lewis, central in the islands, they planned to head for Oban, further southwest in Scotland and get the ferry to Castlebay on the Isle of Barra at the base of the Islands and start their trek heading north from there. You will just be able to make out Oban at the bottom of the map (on page 11) on the Scottish mainland and Castlebay on the isle of Barra at the foot of the Outer Hebrides. Tickets were changed at Piccadilly station for the new route, Manchester to Oban via Glasgow. They both had a £30 Railcard that would save themselves a chunk of money across the whole return trip to Scotland. They had each previously purchased a £62 return ticket Manchester to Glasgow Central and then a £146 return ticket to Fort William. With their Railcards (over 60's senior) this had brought the £146 each down to £96. Just one leg of the journey had paid for the Railcard straightaway. They then changed that to a one-way ticket from Glasgow - Queen Street to Oban at £16 single. They were not on the clock in the way that they constructed this adventure but they had to be mindful of two dates. They had booked to stay one night in the Bothy at Eagles Nest on 21st May (2 weeks away yet) so they must be in Mangersta on the west coast of the Isle of Lewis by 21st May to ensure that they were there in time to experience the famous Bothy for one night. After that anything was possible across the rest of their time providing they were in Glasgow by 6th June to meet the terms of their return ticket to Manchester. Anything else was completely fluid. The train journey from Piccadilly to Glasgow lasted three and a half hours but passed fairly quickly and was full of great views of the North West coast of England and the South West of Scotland. The train made about five stops on the way including Preston and Carlisle and eventually arrived around 12.30pm at Glasgow Central Station. The lads then made the ten-minute walk to Glasgow Queen Street Station and boarded the train to Oban which was another three hour plus journey despite there being less than 100 miles to cover. The train journey however was more than spectacular. It has a renowned reputation of having one of the most scenic train journeys in the world and although quite a boast, it didn't disappoint. It also had a bar and café on it, so no complaints from the duo regarding the length of the journey as all of this more than made up for it. The train's main route was cost effectively managed too with six Carriages travelled from Glasgow to Oban, then four of them on to Fort William and then the final two on to Mallaig on

HEBRIDEAN HOSPITALITY

the coast. Arriving at Oban the lads had just two priorities and they were to get their Ferry tickets sorted for the following day's travel and to find their B&B.

They sorted their ferry tickets easily enough and booked on to two ferries. The first was from Oban the following morning over to Castlebay on the island of Barra. Then a second ferry ticket from Barra to Eriskay on South Uist costing a total of £19 each just the one way, which was very reasonable.

Their back up plan was to kip in the ferry port at Oban but they had managed to book the local B&B in advance of the trip which was at the top of the town called 'The Cullen House Hotel'

With the security of a room for the night and the promise of a hearty breakfast, they headed for a Wetherspoons they had spotted on the way to the B&B. The plan was a few pints of Guinness and a bite to eat. They recall now that in fact they both drank in excess of a gallon of the black stuff that night and finished off with Fish and Chips. Fish and Chips was an understatement too. In Manchester, where Fish & Chips are seen as a local dish, there are a good few chip shops like 'Hills Chippy' in Middleton, that are renowned for their prize-winning Fish and Chips and that you would send any visitor to in order to sample the food that a lot of Mancunians love. This Fish & Chips in Oban was something else again. It looked like Moby dick had been fried. It wasn't just hanging off the plate, it was hanging off the table! Well, maybe a slight exaggeration but it was huge.

Photo: The first Guinness at Oban in sight of the Ferry

What a first night away. They may not have left the mainland yet but they felt their adventure had well and truly begun. The most unusual thing of the first night however wasn't the size of the fish or the fact that they drunk enough Guinness to sink a battleship, it was the expense. They had a budget for the first night which included provision for a B&B and for the food and drink. The first night of any trip tends to be the most expensive as you adjust to your surroundings and then try and save a few bob as you go on.

They started the night with a very generous £100 Kitty between them for the food and drink. After drinking what they believe was in excess of ten pints of Guinness and wolfing down the gigantic fish and chips, they counted the money they had left in the kitty and there was £70.

How on earth did that happen? They scratched their heads. Did some locals treat them to a few pints? Were they charged the full amount for the grub? Who knows?

This was going to be a great trip if this carried on. What they didn't know as they prepared for the next morning and the ferry trip from Oban to Barra, was that the generosity of the locals on the Hebridean Islands was going to outstrip anything they had ever come across.

Photo: The Ferry from Oban to Castlebay, Barra.

HEBRIDEAN HOSPITALITY

Map of The Outer Hebrides & Mainland Scotland

(maps of the islands in the order of travelling North are at pages 78 -84)

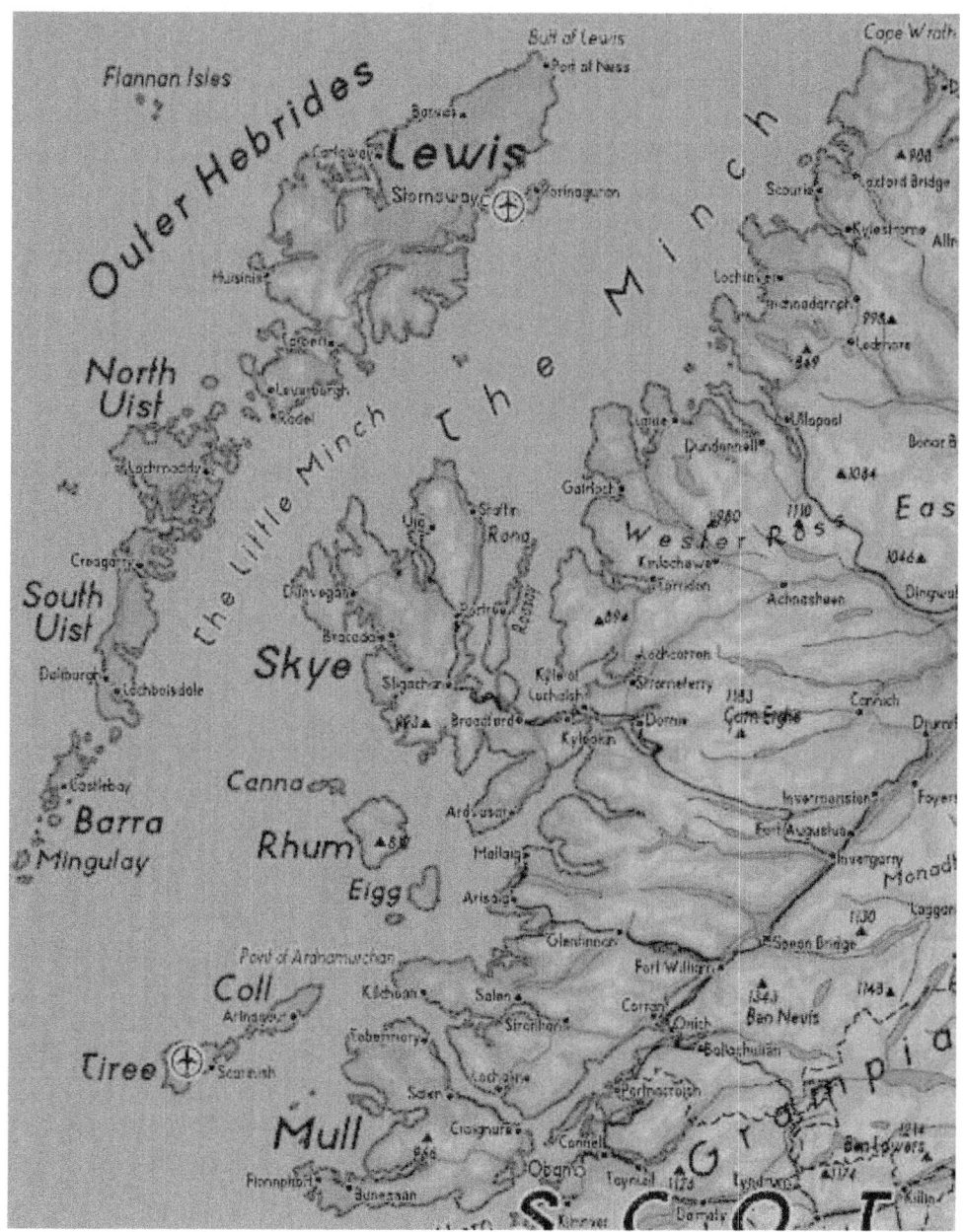

Day 2 – Oban to Barra - Sunday 8th May

They woke up to a beautiful morning on day two at The Cullen House Hotel. A shower and a shave later, the lads were downstairs. The place was beautifully clean and had provided a very good quality bed and breakfast for just £51 for the two of them. Both of the lads took the opportunity to speak to the lady owner and tell her what a credit the place was to her. If the hospitality and standards on the island were anything like they were there in Oban then they were in for a huge treat.

They walked into Oban centre to get breakfast and arrived just in time to see a piper come down a hill in the town leading with 200 cyclists behind him and turned left going out of town. What a sight to behold. They tried to find out what later what it was but with no luck. They speculated it was either a memorial tribute to a cyclist that had died or a ceremony to launch a race.

Breakfast became their next mission so they headed for Wetherspoons. Full Scottish, just the job, and refills as many times after. So after about 4 gallons of coffee (only a slight exaggeration) the lads found themselves at the Ferry Port, thinking they would have to wait a while for the Ferry over to the islands. It couldn't have fallen better. No real waiting time at all for the ferry to Castle Bay, Barra at 1:10 pm. It wasn't a rough crossing but it wasn't a millpond either. These big ferries have powerful stabilisers so it's hard to remember you are on a ship at times. and it was such a nice day.

The weather was going to change though and change dramatically but more on that shortly. The journey took just over four and a half hours. On arrival at Castlebay, they started to look for their next place to stay for the night so that they could prepare for a fresh start on their journey across the islands the next day. Castlebay was like a fishing village and after a look around it was clear that there was not an awful lot by way of places to stay. It was now early evening and raining and they still hadn't found anywhere. They eventually received an offer of sleeping in a shed in 'The Dunard Hostel'. Now Chris has vast experience of sleeping in a shed and if this was the best they could do then so be it so Chris accepted saying it was fine. Harry was a little more apprehensive about it. His exact words were in fact 'No Way'. It turned out it wasn't just a simple shed. It was a shed, within another shed within a garage. Or as Chris referred to it 'luxury – your own shed with an ensuite Shed'. Harry still wasn't convinced but they parked their backpacks and headed the local Co-op to get some food and drink for the evening. They returned to the hostel with Pizzas and beer and after preparing their food in the communal kitchen, they socialised with the other guests in the hostel's lounge. Their fellow travellers in the hostel were kind and hospitable and they made the lads feel very welcome. They must have spoken to about ten people. They were all Scottish and all cyclists. They played music and some of the girls danced and it was a really pleasant and peaceful atmosphere.

The Hostel was owned by Chris and Katie. Chris spoke to Harry and said that if he wanted to sleep on the sofa he could. Harry was very happy to take him up on the offer.

Two days in and Chris is staying in a luxury shed and Harry is on a sofa bed that's actually just a sofa but both lads confirm that they were still cock-a-hoop at the way the locals and fellow travellers were treating them so well and genuinely trying to help them already.

Photo: Castlebay, Barra

Day 3 – Castlebay (Barra) to Eriskay - Monday 9th of May

Chris had slept like a log and Harry had enjoyed a warm comfortable night, even allowing for the several visits to the loo a man of a certain age might make in the night. They packed and enjoyed a coffee before leaving. The weather outside had taken a real turn and it was now gale force conditions. As they walked out of Castlebay they were being pummelled by the rain and the force of the wind. Poor Harry was literally wet through and they'd only walked a few miles. Chris however was faring a lot better and was dry as a bone underneath his clothing. The difference was in the clothing they had invested in. Harry had bought himself a £35 pair of waterproof pants from a well-known outdoor clothing range that really looked the part. £35 certainly doesn't feel you've scrimped over the cost and you would expect them to do what they purported to do, which was to be waterproof. The only problem was that they were shower proof but were not gale proof. Chris, however, had 'Paramo' and 'Himalayo' clothing which are some of the best on the market. Waterproof pants would set you back around £260 and had been tried and tested against the worst elements. Brands like these do exactly what it says on the tin. When buying clothing for these sort of elements, you have to know what you are looking for and what you want it to do. The lads walked about 2 to 3 miles to the Isle of Barra Beach Hotel. They asked about a bus and it turned out to be about three hours away from arriving. They had a coffee and spoke to the lady that owned the hotel, a lovely lady named Joan and also a chap called Eugene who was her right-hand man. In the conversation Chris mentioned about his book and Joan and Eugene asked for a photo with them as they thought what they were doing was inspirational. The lads clicked with these people straightaway. The phrase ' treat others how you would expect to be treated yourself' is commonly used in life but not always adhered to. Harry and Chris came to understand that the islands were full of people who adopted this attitude and applied it daily. The lads were being treated properly as guests of their island. Joan phoned a taxi firm for a price which turned out to be £15 to get to the next ferry going from Ardnam ferry Port to the Isle of Eriskay. The lads agreed that was the best option given the weather. They arrived in time at Ardnam to get the 11.20am ferry, even though they were booked on the 3:45 pm. Had they continued to walk, if they made it in time for the later ferry they would have been in a mess with their gear due to the terrible wind and rain. The Ferries between the islands were much smaller and held a handful of vehicles and about 20 passengers. The journey was only 20 minutes but was choppy with extremely poor visibility.

Arriving on the island of Eriskay and experiencing the conditions, both Harry and Chris both hit a point of realisation of where they were. The gale force conditions, the nature of the place and the rawness of the sea and the terrain hit home that Manchester was hundreds of miles away and they were here now in the Outer Hebrides . They loved it. This is why they had come here, to experience the environment and its conditions. They were like two kids on an adventure. Other people, mostly cyclists, were passing them and looking at them as if they were two supermen carrying around a small car on their backs. As soon as they arrived at Eriskay they walked about two miles all uphill and found a pub called the AM Politician, named after the ship, the 'SS Politician' that ran aground in 1941 and inspired the film 'Whisky Galore'.

The 'SS Politician' - It was February 1941 when the SS Politician set sail from Liverpool heading to Jamaica and New Orleans with cargo that included over a quarter of a million bottles of whisky. As she passed near the Hebrides she hit a gale, much like Harry and Chris had, and after a struggle by the captain to keep the ship on its course she ended up running aground on the banks of Eriskay. The story goes that the lifeboat crew based on Barra were given the incorrect location of the ship due to the fact that it had run off its course. Locals of Eriskay began a rescue of the crew as the ship was taking on water and began to flood. Eventually all the crew were rescued but when the local Islanders learned exactly from the crew what the ship was carrying, a series of illegal salvage operations took place during the night before customs officials arrived. No duty had been paid on the bottles of whisky and therefore customs would have been very keen to get hold of this cargo. Boats came from as far away as Lewis once word was out about what was happening. A legal Argument then ensued about the legal ownership of the cargo. The whole story is told in the film 'Whisky Galore' and is known world-wide now. The wreck of the ship is of course still there but no longer visible. In 1987 a local man found another eight bottles in the wreck and sold them at auction for £4,000. In 1988 Eriskay got its first 'legal' pub and named it 'AM Politician' after the famous ship. Visitors can now enjoy a welcome drink in their bar and restaurant and hear the full story there and they even have a few relics and images on display. The pub is also now known for its' warm welcome and first class food.

So back to our intrepid heroes - The AM Politician was a welcome sight for the lads getting shelter and warmth from the gale outside but the warmest feeling came from the welcome they received from locals and especially Natalie, who worked behind the bar. After introduction and hearing Chris and Harry's story, Natalie rang around all the B&B's on Eriskay looking for a place for the lads to stay the night. She eventually found them a place in a hostel type building for £25 each on a campsite at West Kilbride where you also had access to kitchen facilities. During normal working hours there was also a café for breakfast and dinner if that's what any guest wanted. The bus out to the hostel set them back £1.60 each for just the single journey as Natalie had even arranged to for the lads to be picked up from the campsite where the hostel was and brought back to the AM Politician for 6.45pm. The hostel turned out to be more than acceptable. The place was clean and provided perfect facilities given that it was only £25 per night. They dried themselves and unpacked to let everything dry out. It's a sensible suggestion for anyone visiting the islands, to try and book places in advance. The lads had one or two panicky days where there was nowhere to pitch a tent or the weather was bad enough that they needed a B&B and they'd left it until the last minute. They were very fortunate to get some help along the way. The taxi came and picked them up and they sat down to a fantastic evening meal in the AM Politician of fresh scallops. Harry said the best way to describe the scallops was "Wow". They were huge and were top quality. He had no doubt that the £20 he paid for them would have been £35-£50 in a top restaurant back in Manchester. They had a few beers and got talking to a lovely couple. After a moment Harry said "I know you" and the chap smiled back at him. Later that evening, Harry said to Chris "you know who that was don't you?" "Who?" said Chris. "It's Dave Whelan who used to own Wigan Football club. Well it's either him or his doppelganger" said Harry. Chris went outside to try and see the guy's vehicle. It was a Range Rover and the reg included DWJ so they thought that it must be him or was it a huge coincidence? The chap, whoever he was, was very modest and down to earth. They decided not to mither him about who he was as he clearly was enjoying a peaceful break on the islands. Two very kind people who were staying on the same campsite gave the lads a lift back and that night the lads made a big decision. The weather was bad and looked like it could continue like that, so they formed a plan regarding their intentions going forward. Their plan was to wild camp every night if they could but that if the weather continued as it was, they would ensure they were sleeping under shelter of a B&B or Hostel. It was a big influence on what they did as it turned out because they never really hit great weather again other than about four days across the remainder of their time on the islands. Their previous gung-ho attitude was now being managed more sensibly.

They were now convinced that they had to show the Hebridean weather more respect and also that their experiences of meeting local people whilst in and out of B&B's and local pubs was just as important as anything they were doing. The people they were meeting were the salt of the earth and the lads couldn't believe just how welcome they were being made to feel so many hundreds of miles away from home.

Photo: Chris with actual flare gun from the SS Politician

Day 4 – Eriskay to Benbecula Tuesday 10th of May

The next day, they headed for breakfast and had both agreed that if they saw 'Dave Whelan' or his look alike they would ask him directly about who he was as it was driving them mad with intrigue. Unfortunately, this never happened.

The weather was showing signs that it was going to be as atrocious as the previous day. The wind was up and it was raining on and off. They headed over to the camp café and spoke to a lady cyclist. She was in her 60's and was cycling the islands alone. They met so many inspirational people like this on the islands. The place seemed to attract such interesting and amazing people.

That said, the islands felt a very safe place for people to travel alone. People were definitely looking out for you and you would never feel alone from one place to the next. If someone was alone, or not for that matter, and struggling, the islanders had a knack of spotting it and coming to your assistance. More of that later.

The lads also talked to four lads that morning who had all either been in the RAF or still were. They were also braving the elements and cycling from one island to the next. They had listened to Chris and Harry for a while and said to them "you are ex forces aren't you?" In unison, Harry and Chris had replied "No we're just two lunatics"

As they were enjoying breakfast a chap caught their attention and came over to have a chat with them. His introduced himself to the lads and they did the same. His name was Roy Theobold. He was a professional Toastmaster / Master of Ceremonies based in the south of England and mostly operated in and around London. He had presided over some pretty big events and met some amazing and some very high-profile people.

They chatted but Harry was getting distracted and was eyeing Roy's sausages up. Roy spotted this and duly obliged by encouraging Harry to help himself to one. They had known each other five minutes and were already sharing food.

Both Harry and Chris enjoyed Roy's company immensely and he was fascinated by them. They hit it off perfectly and were genuinely interested in each other's background and stories. This was the sort of thing that just happened on the islands. It wasn't commercialised and nobody was trying to sell you anything. People who they met there were of like mind and everyone had time for each other.

It was the polar opposite of a bustly city where, despite there being thousands of people on the streets, nobody really saw each other, and if they did, it wasn't as an interesting fellow human with their life experiences to share. You need your wits about you in the city and it was nice to relax and let your guard down a little.

Roy was heading back to England as the Queen's Platinum Jubilee celebrations were underway and Roy had an event at the Guild Hall that he was presiding over. That makes it sound very straightforward but it didn't take a lot of investigation online to pick up that this was a dinner for the Lord Mayor. This chap was a seriously successful professional.

Their contact with Roy was brief but extremely interesting and they swapped details for future reference. You just never know when their paths will cross again. Roy's website for anyone interested in the sort of thing he does is: http://www.citytoastmasters.co.uk

The plan for the rest of the day was to get to Benbecula and camp on the beach. They went for the bus which had a stop just outside the site. When the bus pulled up, the driver said "Where are you going to?". Harry said "Benbecula - where are you going to? The driver said "Benbecula it is then" It was £9 each for the journey of 33 Miles north travelling the length of the island of South Uist. It wasn't long after they arrived at Benbecula that they realised that they had left their walking poles on the Bus. This is where Chris's high standard of gear costs him more than Harry. Chris left £130 worth of poles on the bus and Harry left £50 worth of poles. Harry said how pleased he was that he'd saved a fortune! They both saw the funny side of it and moved on.

They didn't chase the matter or make any calls about where the poles may have end up. They'd rather think of it that some lucky visitors to the islands would get some brand-new walking poles courtesy of the Scary Hikers. Chris did rue the fact that he spent so much on them and Harry commented that for the price Chris had paid, he would have wanted them to have homing devices on them!

So here they were in Benbecula where they had heard a lot about the famous sand dunes and sandy beach. They popped into a store called MacLeans Bakery which boasted to be the master bakers of Benbecula. They bought food and drink from MacLeans and the local supermarket and headed towards the site. The Isle of Barra Hotel had kindly gifted to them an Isle of barra hotel waterproof bag which was now full and hanging around Chris's neck as they yomped to where they would pitch their tents on the beach for the night.

Photo: Benbecula Beach (Shadow of the tents and the lads themselves)

They set up camp and pitched their tents in the dunes to give them some protection from the elements. They had bought their tents in the same way that they had bought their waterproofs and they're walking poles. Harry had bought a brand new tent costing £155 from Go Outdoors and Chris had bought an Agnes Wall tent for £400. Both did the trick in this case but the biggest tip here though is provided by Chris.

Before you ever set off to go camping, you have a dry run of putting your tent up under no pressure in your garden or nearby. You answer two important questions in doing that: 'Have I got a mental picture of what I'm putting together here?' and 'have I got all the right components? In addition, you will know how long it takes you to set up the tent which is invaluable information when working in bad weather.

As they finished the set up they collected rocks and heavy pebbles and driftwood to make a small wall around each the tent to weigh them down just to make sure as the wind was picking up again. They had fears that both of them could end up as Zeppelins flying around the islands that night.

As they had both had a healthy cooked breakfast that day, it was ham on cobs with crisps for evening meal and then a walk along the beach behind the airport.

The weather closed in so they returned to their tents just as the rain came down. The main thing was that they were dry and had managed to get fully set up with their sleeping bags and mattresses before the heavens opened.

The night was full of dramatic winds 40 to 50 mph and heavy rain and they were awoken several times but the tents did their job and extra weight they had placed strategically around them to give them extra protection from the weather, meant they had remained dry and survived the night.

Photo: The lads prepare to brave the winds on Benbecula beach.

Day 5 – Benbecula to Willie's House - Wednesday, the 11th of May

The lads were relieved to wake to calm weather and sunshine and the sound of breaking waves on the seashore. There wasn't a soul in sight and the fresh air was just amazing. They tidied the tent and got organised. When they had finished, there was a guy walking along the beach with his dog which looked like a cross between a Bull Mastiff and a Rottweiler. They said hello and asked him about any community facilities to have a wash in and where to get some breakfast. They couldn't have asked a better person. His name was Willie Irvine from Dundee and he would be instrumental in bringing Chris out of his two-year retirement.

When Willie heard that the lads needed breakfast, a shower and freshen up, he immediately gave them directions. Well maybe not directions but more like instructions. They had never met this man before but this is exactly what he said:-

" Walk north to the main road and turn left. Walk for about half an hour and you will come to Charlie's bistro. You will get a wonderful full breakfast in there and then in about 1 ½ hours I will pick you up, as I am going that way, and take you to my house so you can have a shower and get organised'

... and that is exactly what happened. Amazing!. On the way to his house, Willie asked where the lads were sleeping that night. Harry said " A field or a beach when we find one". "No" Willie said " You can pitch your tents on my lawn" and so we did. Willie was on the islands renovating a house that he had bought there.

After our showers, Willie asked "have you got some beers with you?" Chris said "yes we have" Willie then brought out a bottle of Jura whisky from the isle of Jura in the Inner Hebrides. They had an absolutely brilliant night telling each other tales and roaring laughing as they drunk the whisky and the beer. When the second bottle of Jura came out it wasn't long before Chris didn't so much go to sleep but just tilted to one side and was out for the count. Willie threw a quilt over him where he was and said "Let him sleep peacefully where he is". Harry bid Willie goodnight and made his way to his tent in the garden. Everyone slept like logs and Chris and Harry were very much appreciative of this genial guy they had randomly bumped into on the beach only that morning.

HEBRIDEAN HOSPITALITY

Day 6 - Benbecula to Loch Maddy - Thursday 12th of May

The next morning, Willie had cooked them both a hearty breakfast. What a guy. Harry and Chris just couldn't believe that they could keep meeting such kind and welcoming people. It was clear that Willie had thoroughly enjoyed their company too. As said earlier, Willie was from Dundee. He was a roofer by trade and he and his partner had been looking for two years for a property on the Islands. The building they had bought used to be a B&B and was the building they were now in . Willie had stayed there for three months to do it up while his Mrs (partner) was in Dundee. He was right in the middle of his three month work project. As Chris and Willie talked it became apparent that they had both been out in New Zealand at the same time watching the Rugby world cup back in 2003. Who knows, their paths may have already crossed.

Little pieces of the conversation were so funny and amazing at the same time and just gave glimpses of the differing lifestyles of people in The Outer Hebrides to people on the mainland. Willie told them of the time that he had said to one of his neighbours on the island "You won't believe this but I saw a Golden Eagle this morning" and the islander would say "I know. They are a bloody nuisance aren't they?"

Another morning Willie had said that he heard a tapping on the window and it was a Deer tapping its antlers on his window. He realised that the Deer could see its own reflection in the window and was playfully clashing antlers with its' new imaginary friend. It made Chris giggle just recounting these stories

Before the lads left, Willie, having learnt that Chris was now a retired barber, convinced Chris to give him a haircut. Chris hadn't given anyone a haircut for over two years and had left the trade, believing he would never cut hair again. It doesn't sound like such a big deal but to understand Chris was to understand what a major thing this was. When you have had a brain injury and you still suffer the effects of that, a simple activity that you have done for over forty years but have not done for a short time, even weeks, becomes a very big mental challenge. What was happening to Chris in the Islands was that he was meeting so many people of like mind who were not commercial in any way or who had any angle when they made offers of kindness other than kindness itself. Chris was so chilled by this time, that when Willie produced a pair of clippers and scissors, Chris's reaction was "with pleasure" and he proceeded to cut Willie's hair. Chris said afterwards that "it was a real privilege to give him a haircut and I'd not felt like doing that for a long time. I was so happy to do it even though I'd swore to myself that I would never cut hair again"

Photo: 'Anything for the weekend sir? Chris cuts Willies hair.

HEBRIDEAN HOSPITALITY

So, they left Willie's house about 11am. They said their goodbyes and swore that one day they would return to see Willie and his partner and their completed house.

They walked one hundred yards to the main road, turned left and then walked solidly for four hours along moorland roads in the direction of Grimsay, described as the largest of the stepping stones islands.

Then, their first real setback of the trip. Harry was struggling with a badly swollen ankle. Sometimes, despite the determination of a person, an ailment can get so bad that it becomes physically impossible to continue to place so much pressure on a joint. Harry, who was in his late 70's, had been carrying around this 30 Kilogram weight (four and a half Stones) on his shoulders and an old ankle injury had reared its head. He had been suffering for a while but had not mentioned anything to Chris.

Chris, in the meantime, had been very worried about Harry and the demands being placed on him but neither had said a word. It was the classic Men's mental health issue. It only needed a hint from one to the other and they would have stopped and reviewed their predicament. Instead, Harry probably covered several kilometres in absolute agony before the joint just couldn't stand the weight anymore.

As soon as Harry mentioned it to Chris, they stopped at a nearby bus stop and decided to rest and discuss it. Chris was almost relieved that Harry had said something because he knew there was a problem and didn't want to dent Harry's pride. Harry on the other hand, waited until the joint was in much worse condition than it needed to be. \

What is it about men's mentality that prevents them from speaking up early on in a problem that can be avoided? There have been many times in history where speaking up may have made such a difference to situations faced by many that may have been avoided. As Mancunians it brings to mind the Munich Air disaster. There are not many people in the world who are not aware that in 1958 Manchester United lost some glorious young men and talented footballers travelling back from a game in Europe through Munich airport. Unless you've read about the events you may not be aware that the plane attempted to take off three times because of ice on the wings. Several of the surviving players admitted by the 3rd attempt they were extremely nervous about the whole situation. It would have only taken one person, just one person, any of the players or even any of the journalists on board to have said " No, I'm not travelling it's too risky" and there would have been an immediate swell of support from most of the team and it would have gone down as a minor story of European football that Manchester United risked a fine from the Football authorities for not being able to fulfil their weekend fixture back home because of flying back late. Instead, what happened effected so many and especially those young players who lost their lives in the prime of their careers destined for so much.

In this case thankfully it wasn't life or death but it was certainly Harry's physical health that was suffering. They sat in the bus stop chatting about what they would do to get to their next stopping point and had made a joint decision that it was going to be buses and ferries from here on in. Just as they agreed that this was the way forward, a bus pulled up on the opposite side of the road but going the other way.

"Are you ok lads" shouted the driver as he wound down his window. "Not really' shouted Harry. "My ankle is playing up and we are heading North" The bus driver just as a natural reaction said "I'm on a school bus run but will be passing back this way about twenty past four. Hang on there and I'll pick you up" He then drove off. Chris turned to Harry and said "In Manchester, how many times have you seen some poor sod running to catch a bus and the driver driving off because they have not made it to the bus stop yet? Here, they chase after you even when you haven't put your hand out!!"

Sure enough, around twenty past four, the driver returned, but he was no longer driving a minibus, he came back with a 72-seater coach carrying school kids. As they boarded the coach the driver said to the duo "We are heading to Lochmaddy" Harry replied "Lochmaddy is on the Eastside and we need to be in Berneray on the north side for the ferry to Harris" "No problem" said the driver "where I am going to drop you, a yellow minibus will be waiting to take you to Berneray" Chris and Harry looked at each other as if to ask; "Were everyone on these islands the most helpful people in the world?" And sure enough they were!

The coach was filled with school kids on the school run home but there were also a few shoppers being dropped off and shopping itself being dropped off for people, who the lads were guessing, couldn't get out of the house. When they arrived at Lochmaddy there was the yellow minibus waiting for the lads just as the driver had said it would be. Only Harry and Chris got off which meant this particular stop off had been just for them. They went to pay the driver and he waved them away. This was a ten mile trip and they had gone out of their way to help the lads and didn't want anything in return.

The lady driver of the yellow minibus told us that the driver of the coach had radioed ahead earlier and asked her to wait to make sure that they made the ferry. She dropped the lads at the Lochmaddy Ferry in time for them to board the 5.45pm boat to Leverburgh on the island of Harris.

The crossing took about an hour and the lads met several people who exchanged experiences with them about the islands as they too headed for Leverburgh but had all booked B&Bs for the night. They started to think they should have booked ahead themselves.

They disembarked from the ferry and walked towards what they thought would be the village attached to the ferry port. In reality they came across two rows of cottages one of which was a bed and breakfast. They knocked on the door and spoke to the woman who run the B&B and she broke it to them that she had no vacancies. However, in keeping with the helpfulness of everybody they had met so far, she telephoned around to see if anywhere else further afield had any vacancies but with no joy. The lads decided to return to the ferry terminal as they had seen that the waiting room in the terminal was warm and had toilet facilities. They decided that, given the hour and the atrocious weather outside that the waiting room seemed like a viable option for the night.

As it turned out timing of this decision was crucial. The lads walked back to the Ferry terminal in what they described as a howling gale with the rain almost horizontal and had no sooner entered the warm waiting room and shut the door behind them when they heard a loud click coming from the door.

As they both looked back, they saw a sign that said "This door automatically locks at 7pm and will not re-open until 7am. Now there would be some people that would call that false imprisonment. There would be others who would panic and start banging on the doors and windows, especially the claustrophobics. What did Harry and Chris do? They cheered and hugged each other. Why? Well because they had just secured a private and warm room for the night away from the rain and wind. They were safe and secure from any interruption in this perfect overnight room. They blew up their inflatable mattresses, made their beds for the night and then got out their portable cooking rings and started to make their evening meal of coffee and green tea with cheese and ham sandwiches and shortbread biscuits.

"Luxury" said Chris "5 star" said Harry chuckling away to themselves and chatting into the night about whether they could get the Ferryport Waiting Room on to Trip Advisor. and staring out the window at the horrendous night of bad weather that they were now protected from. Chris said "In Manchester a 'Lock in' is totally different but this is just as good" What's more this was entirely free of charge.

Photo: The Locked Waiting Room at Leverburgh, Harris

Day 7 – Leverburgh to Tarbert - Friday 13th May

In the morning, they woke fresh from a long and restful sleep. They let their mattresses down and packed everything away. They stood by the door and with military precision the door clicked open promptly at 7:00 am. The lads walked straight across the road to a 'butty bus' which was parked up outside the Ferry terminal and both of them had a bacon barm and a coffee. Life felt good. It was still raining, although not as heavy as the night before, so they decided to get the 9.00am bus to Tarbert which was about 22 miles northeast as they travelled up Harris towards Lewis. People commonly think that Harris and Lewis are two different islands in the Outer Hebrides but in fact they are one land mass. The lads travelled the length of Harris to get to Tarbert and Tarbert is at the Southern edge of Lewis. £4.20 for a bus ticket taking you 22 miles wasn't half bad at all. The lads were delighted with the way their money was stretching but they knew that a lot of that was down to the hospitality of the Hebridean people. The islands were so user friendly with their prices and their flexibility. The bus driver was a great guy who made you feel very welcome and helpfully gave us information along the way. The journey of two hours included picking people up in what seemed to us like the middle of nowhere, including two ladies that we had met on the ferry who were also going to Tarbert. It was a small world on the islands.

Photo: Harry looks cool but is desperately holding on for fear of being blown away

HEBRIDEAN HOSPITALITY

They arrived at Tarbert and immediately made their way to an ATM for cash. They wandered around a little looking for a base for a couple of days but there was nothing doing. They eventually go into a grocery shop and asked the owner if he knew anybody that rented out rooms and just by chance he said, "We have a flat upstairs and rent it out" He took us up and it was a three-bedroom flat with kitchen, bathroom, lounge and dining room. He said "I charge £150 per night". Chief negotiator Harry said "Can you do three nights?" but the guy said he could only rent it out for two nights Friday and Saturday. Harry asked 'Can you do it for the two nights for £200?" The owner replied with "I can do it for £240" and that was it. They had a deal and a fair one at that.

By this time, six days into the trip and Harry's ankle was still troubling him and his left heel had blistered badly. The bag was so heavy for him to cope with that the lads agreed to recharge their batteries and dry out and relax for the two days. There were no pubs in the vicinity that the lads would recognise as pubs but there were a few hotels with their own bars. They ventured out first at lunchtime to 'The Hotel Hebrides' and enjoyed three pints of the black stuff each and shared a pizza with chips costing them £43 which was very reasonable. They headed back to the flat, had a hot bath and a kip for a couple of hours then got ready to head out again. By the time Harry had woken and got ready, Chris had already been out and come back, the new owner of a Harris Tweed hat. At 6.00pm they started at a hotel nearby called 'The Harris Hotel' and after a couple of pints there headed back to The Hotel Hebrides' where it seemed a lot of people gathered and there was a bit of an atmosphere. The lads met a guy called Brian from Kendall who was walking the 'Hebridean Way' on his own and invited the lads to join him. They chatted for hours. The 'Hebridean way' is a set walk of 156 miles from Vatersay to Stornaway and encompasses 10 islands, crossing 6 causeways and two ferry rides, much of which Chris and Harry would experience themselves on their own journey. By 10pm they had downed a few more Guinness's and shared another pizza. Bearing in mind Chris normally hits the sack by 7pm when at home and is up well before the larks, this was a heck of a night out for him. They walked back to the flat reflecting on the night and immediately went to bed, although Harry managed also to get a wash on for his smalls and dry some clothes on the radiator before retiring. No rest for the wicked.

HEBRIDEAN HOSPITALITY

Day 8 - Tarbert - Saturday, the 14th of May

Up and at 'em the next morning, the lads went into the shop and got eggs, butter and scotch rolls and had egg on toast. "Luxury" says Harry. Chris had a hot bath and loved it. This was the life.

They walked to the Harris Tweed shop and bought another hat each before setting off to visit a place that they had heard of from locals as a great place to visit, the Isle of Harris Distillery which was based in Tarbert. It became clear on the tour that there would be no whisky tasting but they would be sampling the very popular gin. They asked the tour guide why they were selling gin in a whisky distillery. The guy told them that the place was only six years old so no whisky has been sold yet as it was still maturing but in the meantime they were also producing gin. The whisky would not be sold until a team of very experienced tasters decided when the whisky was ready for drinking. The lads really enjoyed the tour and the gin and would recommend it to anyone visiting.

They then went to the shop and bought beers for the fridge back at the flat and then off they went back to the Hebridean Hotel for a Guiness. They met a lad called Alex who had been travelling around the world for the last six years. After a brief chat it was clear they got on and they arranged to meet on the Monday evening at O'Neills bar in Stornoway, where the lads had now decided to make their next base. Stornaway was the ideal place for them to plan various trips out from but have a base for their gear. The lads also spoke to a lad from Whalley Range of all places, who was a consultant in acoustics. It seemed wherever they went they were making friends with people who were genuinely interested in what they were doing on the islands and the people themselves all had interesting background stories themselves.

Around 6.00pm they left the pub to run up the hill to order fish and chips at the Mobile van for 7 o'clock. They went back to the pub to watch the end of the FA Cup Final between Chelsea and Liverpool and then back to the van for fish and chips where Chris struck up a conversation with a chap called Alan who had been a sound engineer with the Beatles. There was no end to a long line of fascinating people on these islands. They went back to the flat and ate their supper with a few beers then hit the sack around 9.00pm. The trip was getting better and better and certainly less painful for Harry at this stage with less trekking carrying the heavy rucksack.

HEBRIDEAN HOSPITALITY

Day 9 - Tarbert to Stornaway - Sunday, the 15th of May

Sunday was going to be a little different. They woke around 8.00am, Bath / Shower and shave (for Harry) and then it was a cheese roll and a couple of green teas for them both for breakfast. They left the flat at around 10:30am loaded with their rucksacks and off they set to find somewhere to wild camp for the night on the Stornaway Road. Their plan was to get the legs going again but they didn't want to push things with Harry's ankle. There were no buses to Stornaway until the next day, Monday, and so they would wild camp for Sunday night. Just a couple of miles out of town they spotted an ideal field with some sheep overlooking the spectacular Loch Seaforth. Big blue water heading out to sea with islands dotted around on one side and mountains on the other. What better place to set up camp. They completed the task and then treated themselves to two more cheese and crisp rolls and a couple of boiled eggs and a chocolate biscuit, every bite tasted like the food of Kings as they sat admiring the scenery bathed in blue sky and sunshine. They relaxed with a few cans of Guiness to help them wind down until eventually turning in around 8pm to ensure they were fresh for the next morning. It wasn't long before they were in their tents and out like a light.

Photo: Camp at Loch Seaforth

HEBRIDEAN HOSPITALITY

Photo: Chris at Loch Seaforth

Day 10 – The Road to Stornaway – Monday 16th May

They were both up and awake at 6:30am. They packed up and walked back to Tarbert to get breakfast and get the bus to Stornaway. The food van didn't open on Mondays so that they could clean and stock up but the lads spoke with the owners and had a photo taken with them anyway.

They then waited for the bus to Stornoway which arrived around 9:45 am. They had tried to get some more money from ATM but the ATM had no money till the van came over on the ferry from Skye. This tickled the lads as this was in fact the Outer Hebrides that they were expecting and they found it comforting in a way. They were miles from the mainland and in a piece of heaven on these islands.

They caught the bus to Stornoway which was 37 miles away from Tarbert heading Northeast on Harris. That bus was £9.82 each for the journey which was a little steeper than they had paid on other buses but it was still a very reasonable price.

When they reached Stornaway and were unloading, Harry asked the driver where the Laxdale campsite was and he said "that's four of you heading there – get back on the bus and I'll drop you off on the way back" Where he actually dropped them, they had a mile to walk to the site. They paid for five nights Monday to Friday at £14 per head but explained to the Campsite owner that they were heading over to 'Eagles Nest' in Mangersta on Saturday and would like to leave one of the tents up at the site. The owner indicated that there would be no problem with that and no charges either. They pitched their tents then walked back into Stornoway and headed straight for McNeills Bar.

Almost immediately afterwards, Brian from Kendal walked in and they had a pint together before he left after agreeing to meet the lads later in a pub called The Crown Inn in the centre of Stornaway. As he left, he dropped his cap on the floor. Luckily Harry found it before they left.

They walked through the pedestrian parts of town to The Crown Inn where they met Brian again. Brian was staying at the crown for the night and bought the lads a pint (as he had forgotten to pay his bill back in Tarbert!). They laughed about it but at least he got his cap back which he was pleased about.

As they left The Crown, they bumped into a couple they had met enroute to Stornaway. The woman, Sue, was a technical director for athletics and her husband, Darren, had worked for the BBC and then for Formula One racing.

The people the lads were meeting on a daily basis were unbelievable. Such interesting characters. What was drawing them all to these islands?

Photo: Sue & Darren

They decided that an early night was in order so they went for fish and chips from the local chip shop and then popped into the Co-op for food and beers and headed back to the campsite.

They were almost wishing the days to pass quickly now as Eagles Nest wasn't far away. Their ambition to see and experience this Bothy in the cliff face was now only days away and they couldn't wait.

They enjoyed their food and drink and Harry updated his diary and both of them were asleep in their tents by 7.30pm.

Day 11 – Stornaway – Tuesday 17th of May

The Laxdale Camp Site was situated just 5 minutes drive or a 30-minute walk from Stornaway town centre. The lads thought the place was fantastic and just what they wanted. It was a very well organised business and had excellent communal facilities. At the top of the field where the tents were pitched there was a kitchen for use by the campers with two cooking hobs, a microwave, a toaster, fridge, freezer and a sink. The lady who ran the place was called Dianne. Her husband was the local church minister. Her father-in-law was the maintenance man and they ran the place really efficiently. There was even plenty of electrical sockets for charging phones. Across the road from the kitchen there was an amenities building where washing pots and pans and laundry took place. It was like a home from home and very reasonable at £14 per night to pitch your tent.

Both lads were awake by 6.00am and made their way over to the Kitchen and cooked some kippers. They had kippers a few times while they were on the islands. On One occasion two dutch lads showed an interest in what they were having and didn't know that Kippers were in fact smoked Herring. A lot of people don't know that they are one and the same thing. In Arbroath, Scotland, they are referred to as 'Smokies'. They showered and shaved and organised their gear to remain on site while they went into Stornaway for the day. Part of the plan on day 11 was to organise the ferry trip on the first leg of the journey back from the islands which was going to be a stop off on the isle of Skye. On their way into town, they stopped off at the Co-op to buy Harry a pair of crocs for £8 and some burgers to cook for their tea in the evening. They continued into Stornaway's town centre and met Sue and Darren (who were camping on the same campsite). They all went into McNeills for lunch (loose translation – 'a pint') and then the lads headed over to the docks. They took some photographs to send back for Chris's Facebook page and admired a French cruise liner that was in the port and travelling around the Outer Hebrides. They went into the Ferry terminal and purchased two single ferry tickets from Tarbert to Uig on the isle of Skye for one week on Saturday 28th May costing £18 each. They did a little more shopping and popped into the best bar in Stornaway (The Crown Inn) for another pint before heading for the 6.05pm bus back to the campsite. All local buses were £1. Extremely inexpensive compared to back home.

There's not an awful lot that you could teach Chris about Nutrition. He is a big fan of cheese as it gives you the energy that you will need for lifting heavy rucksacks & pints of Guinness. It was Harry though that cooked the burgers and toasted the buns with cheese back at the Kitchen. He put two in tinfoil and hand delivered them to Chris in his tent with a 'Bon Appetit'' Deliveroo also alive and well on the islands, it is just called 'Harry' there. He then returned to make two of his own and sat with a bottle of beer enjoying the very tasty Co-op Burgers and chatting to Matt, who was Ian's son.

Finally, Harry decided to call it a night. He finished his diary entry for the day and made a dash that Linford Christie with a bad ankle would have been proud of, back to his tent through, what was now, heavy rain. The tents stood up to the weather across the night brilliantly. Although Harry had an initial problem earlier in the trip with some of the rods provided with the tent and had to ad lib by bending one or two of them, they were in very good shape literally and keeping out some pretty bad weather.

Photo: Stornoway Docks

Day 12 – Stornaway - Wednesday, the 18th of May

Harry woke at 6.15 am and made his way to the Kitchen where he found Chris having coffee, having been up since 5am, showered and ready before anyone else so much as stirred. They enjoyed a hearty breakfast of sausages, bacon and black budding all courtesy of the Co-op. They then organised their tents and walked into Stornaway. They checked their bank accounts and went to draw £100 out but nothing came out of the magic hole in the wall. Harry stomped into the bank to complain and they said they couldn't help him other than to check whether the money had actually come out of his account. The lads had visions of later on that afternoon some Hebridean person wandering past the bank just as £100 came flying out of the hole in the wall and offered itself to him. As they were making up their own stories of what might happen the person who had chat confirmed that nothing had been drawn out and it was the ATM that was probably empty. The lads agreed that given the character of everyone they had met so far on the islands, there was no one that they begrudged the good fortune if the money did fly out of the wall later on.

They then visited the Tourist board office. Harry had been in touch for information a few times and as you might imagine, they were immensely helpful. Harry had spoken with Karen who worked there and had got to know her quite well without actually meeting so it was great to put a face to a name. The lads also checked on buses for 'Eagles Nest' on Saturday. That was one bus they wouldn't be missing. They also checked for the bus to Tarbert a week on Saturday.

They made their way over to see Lews Castle, just west of Stornaway and across the Bayhead river. Elevated above the town, as most castles are, Lews Castle had been built in 1844-51. It was now a museum amongst other things and has had many uses over the last 171 years, including being a base during the second world war for air and ground crew of a special air squadron of the RAF that flew a fleet of six Supermarine Walrus aircraft which were amphibious reconnaissance planes.

The lads were impressed with the history of the place and how it had been used over the years. The displays were incredible and well worth seeing. The grounds of the castle reminded the lads of Heaton Park back in Manchester, also known to some Manchester locals as 'Chris's office' as he is rarely away from the place and regularly holds court on fitness and dietary advice. The grounds at Lews Castle were being further developed as a golf course and the place is renowned for its University of Historical Research and offers studies into the Gaelic language.

Photo: The Security men at Lews Castle looked friendly enough

They returned to Stornoway town centre and looked for a chemist for iron medication. Although they would refer to it as three pints of Guinness at the Crown Inn.

The Crown also offered free technology lessons as the young lady behind the bar showed Harry how to send his photos via Whatsapp to Leo back at base HQ in Manchester for Chris's Facebook page.

After a few hours in the company of the locals at Crown Inn, they popped into both the Co-op and Tesco (they've all got their relevant deals) and also bought a frying pan.

They walked towards the bus station and they noticed a comical set up of a sign saying 'no smoking' and right next door was the fish smokehouse selling kippers. It struck them as funny.

HEBRIDEAN HOSPITALITY

The next bus was some time away so they walked the mile or so back to camp. And why not, the sun was out and the wind dropped a little. Back at camp, Harry showered and shaved and put some washing on and made tea.

Harry delivered Chris's two burgers cheese in tinfoil again and left Chris with his bottle of beer and his headphones on. Does life get any better? Chris was so chilled and so was his personal butler, waiter, chef and holiday rep, Harry. Harry was loving the Hebridean experience and if Chris was happy then Harry was too.

Harry returned to the kitchen, had his tea and put his washing in the dryer. As he completed his diary for the day, he reflected on some observations he and Chris had made that day. They had been on the islands now for 11 days. They had not heard a single siren, seen no police cars, seen no planes, seen no rubbish on the floor and had seen nobody rushing around against the clock. Every morning seemed like a Sunday morning here. There was nobody stressing out or starting an argument or even looking as if they were in a bad mood. When they returned to Manchester they both thought they would have to go through some sort of compression chamber as it was going to be a real shock to the system walking out of Piccaddilly station back into the Manchester way of life after this. It was 9pm – Harry closed the diary and was soon in the land of nod.

Photo. The road to Stornaway from the camp at Laxdale

HEBRIDEAN HOSPITALITY

Day 13 – Stornaway & The Butt of Lewis - Thursday, 19th of May

Harry woke at 6.00am and Chris was already in the kitchen. He washed and did his usual chores then cooked kippers and poached eggs on toast. The diet Harry had planned on coming to the islands was not looking too good. His target was to have lost a stone by now but in fact he had put a stone on! They got ready and walked into Stornaway. Milling around for a while they ended up popping into a café for a coffee and a banana. Harry had started to feel something a bit troublesome in his right calf muscle almost like cramp but being like they both were, he didn't mention it. He took a couple of photos to send home of some impressive carvings outside the local co-op One of a wooden Bull and another of an old Horse and Cart. As he admired the carvings, there was that pain in the right calf again.

They made their way over to the bus station to check on the 12.30pm bus to The Butt of Lewis which was the most northerly tip of Lewis and therefore the John O Groats of The Outer Hebrides. The lads fancied a trip out to visit the location and also see the famous Lighthouse there. It was apparently the only lighthouse in the UK that hasn't ever been painted the usual white or red and white colours and remains the natural red brick it was built from.

At the bus station they spoke to Ann, the lady in the office there, and she gave them a timetable for the relevant bus both ways. They ended up discussing Chris's book with her, 'Making The Cut', and why they were both on the islands. People were genuinely interested in the lads' back stories and what had brought them to their home. The journey to the Butt of Lewis involved getting a bus to a place called Ness which was about 26 miles north of Stornaway. The driver then pointed the lads in the direction of lighthouse which was another mile and a half walk. It was a strong wind so it felt a little more than the mile and a half by the time they arrived. Visitors could not go in the lighthouse itself so they walked around near the buildings, taking photos of the cliffs and the bays.

At the Lighthouse there was a plaque saying 'the Hebridean way' Apparently, this is the unofficial end of the trek until they get funding from the government to finish it off from Stornoway. Currently, the end of the Hebridean Way is at Lews Castle, where the lads had been earlier in the week, but once the funding has been received, it will extend by another 28 miles to The Butt of Lewis. Another amazing side story in relation to this lighthouse (pictured on page 70) other than the fact that it had been made from red brick and never been painted, came to light after the lads returned home. Chris was walking in Middleton, Manchester many months after the trip and bumped into a chap named Phil who he knew very well, along with his son, Daniel, as they were regular customers of his at Chris's barbers shop over the years. The Father and Son pair own and run the local firm 'Crescent Roofing'. Phil told Chris that their business, Crescent Roofing, had worked on the Lighthouse at The Butt of Lewis many years ago. What an amazing coincidence and one that Chris had never known until he mentioned his and Harry's Hebridean experience to Phil.

They caught the bus at 3:40 pm that dropped them off at 4:45 pm at the end of Laxdale Lane at the camp. Harry took the new frying pan and rehearsed for the big night coming up on Saturday by cooking a paella with pepperoni ,spinach, brown rice and King prawns. As Harry said 'it was superb being modest' and a perfect rehearsal for the real event.

Lazy day tomorrow for them both as they get ready for their big day and night at The Eagles Nest bothy on Saturday. They were asleep in their tents by 7.30pm but there was still another day to go before 'Eagles Nest'. They just couldn't wait.

Photo: The Butt of Lewis

HEBRIDEAN HOSPITALITY

Day 14 – Stornaway - Friday, 20th of May

Harry woke around 6 o'clock and, as was now becoming tradition, Chris was already up and in the Kitchen. Harry decided to cook them both a big breakfast as they had nipped into the Co-op in Stornaway the day before and bought pork sausages, squares of sausage and black puddings. Chris also had fried eggs and Harry had toast with his. That plan to lose a stone was really going west but they were excited and needed to get through this day to get to **TOMORROW – THE BIG DAY & NIGHT..**

They washed up and got ready for the next bus at the bottom of the lane 9:20 am. All they could think of was the plan for the next day. This was why they had come to the Islands in the first place. They had this ambition to spend a night in the Eagles Nest bothy at Mangersta and wanted it to be perfectly planned.

They went into the co-op and Harry already had his menu in his mind that he was going to cook on the fire in the bothy tomorrow night. They bought burgers for their tea later and then it was two trays of prawns, packet pepperoni, spinach, runner beans sprouting broccoli, mange tout and two packs of muscles and brown rice. He was planning a real feast.

They were to leave at midday and couldn't wait. They walked to the bus station and double checked on bus times for the next day and then went over to The Crown Inn. They engrossed themselves in several discussions but can't remember most of them because they were so preoccupied with their excitement about their big day and evening only being less then 24 hours away. They phoned Leo who was just as excited for them and who told them to make sure they got photos. Around 4.30pm they walked back to site. They had arranged with Dianne who ran Laxdale, to have a pod for the night with two single beds in, heating, a microwave and a kettle. This gave them a chance to dry all their gear and pack it away ready for the trip over to Mangersta and Eagles Nest the following day. They wanted everything just right and well organised. Dianne had only charged them £20 for the pod because of their long booking which was so good of her. They got it all done and chilled for a while and ate their burgers while chatting with everyone in the camp's kitchen. Eventually they said their good nights and were tucked up in their beds in their pod for 8.10pm like two children on Christmas Eve. Harry updated the diary briefly for the day and then it was lights out.

HEBRIDEAN HOSPITALITY

Day 15 – Stornaway to Mangersta (Eagles Nest) Saturday, 21st of May

Don't ask the lads what happened on the morning because they were that giddy, their memories of the day only begin with getting on the bus at 12.05pm in Stornaway to head for Mangersta.

The journey was impressive. It was breath taking scenery across the moorland and the mountains made the Pennines look like a local park.

They stopped in the middle of nowhere to let people off with shopping. Some got off to get on minibuses waiting for them to take them on to even more remote places. The trip was a real eye-opener to the lads.

Those people lived a very harsh and isolated existence. They came to beaches with white sands and turquoise waters and delivered fish and black puddings to remote restaurants. The lads were last off at the last stop and had been on the bus for about one and half hours. The fare? £4.90 each! crazy price for the distance covered.

The lads had been sent directions and instructions from the owners when they booked to stay for the night in the bothy for this date.

A bothy is normally a communal place for walkers to use as a refuge from the weather or for the night or to cook food in the middle of nowhere. Eagles Nest was probably the most popular bothy in the UK because of its' uniqueness. It was built by an engineer from Stornaway, completely from rocks and was bedded into the cliff face at Mangersta. The view from its single window was breathtaking. It was something very special and therefore you had to book in advance to stay there, which the lads had done.

They followed the directions sent to them by the owners (who lived locally) from arriving to go to a house at number three. They knocked and no one was in, so they followed the next set of instructions from there and found two bags of wood for fuel for the night and directions across a field with a black and white marker on it then a gate in top corner with a wooden arrow on it and a path leading over to the rocks to the Bothy.

They followed the instructions to the letter and found the entrance. They walked in and put their rucksacks down and just sat there staring all around them – "wow" they both said. It was everything they had expected.

Photo: The way to the Eagles Nest Bothy

For those people reading this that think they may at some stage visit the Eagles Nest, the lads suggest that photos really don't do it justice at all. For those that want to see a little more detail around what it is like, they suggest visiting this film on You Tube:

https://www.youtube.com/watch?v=91Sdp83Ulqs

They both suggest though that nothing replaces seeing it for yourself. The islands are spectacular in many respects but this is really a special spot

They got organised, had a drink then lit the fire and sank a few more drinks then Harry really got the fire going and cooked one lot of muscles then a paella even better than the first one he had cooked on the trip as this one he cooked on the open fire in the Eagles Nest Bothy.

HEBRIDEAN HOSPITALITY

Photo: Harry tucks into the Paella in the Bothy

They hear voices and two men and a woman appeared at the door and they asked them in:.

It was a man and his wife and her dad. Fabio, Carmen and Cameron in that order. Carmen was from Stornoway; her husband Fabio is Italian and her dad was Scottish. They had coffee and the lads stuck with their beers and they took photos together. Just in passing, Carmen told the lads that she had bumped into Ben Fogle in Stornoway that day. Amazing coincidence, as he had inspired Harry to instigate this trip in the first place.

Photo: Cameron, Carmen and Fabio at Eagles Nest

They had a really good chat about where they had all come from and exchanged some stories of their backgrounds. Carmen told them that she had visited the Bothy five times but this was the first time she had seen the fire lit. She thought it was even more magical and was so impressed that Harry had just cooked a paella on it. They shared a coffee, that the visitors had brought and they said they goodbyes and off they went. Such lovely people and a pleasure to spend time with. The trip was full of people like this who you would have happily spent hours with sharing experiences and sometimes picking up tips on other travel experiences.

The lads sank a couple more beers and settled down and slept on their mattresses on the floor (Chris) and on the bench (Harry) and both said the following morning it was the best night's sleep for two weeks.

Photo: The Entrance to Eagle's Nest

Day 16 – Eagles Nest - Sunday, the 22nd of May

They had been asleep by 9.00pm the night before so it was hardly surprising that the lads woke about 4.00am and put a brew on. It was another special occasion so Harry cooked Moules Marinieres (a French recipe for Mussels) for breakfast and made coffee and they chatted about where they were going to sleep tonight.

They were enjoying their stay at the bothy so much that they decided to go over to the owner's house and see if it was booked for a further night and ask if they could stay on as it was still raining.

Around 11:30am they made their way to the house but no one in. They looked for more wood but none to be found. As they made their way back a couple were walking over the fields and said they were going to look at the bothy. They were going to stay but the wife didn't fancy it. This sounded promising. Maybe the bothy would be free for the evening.

As the evening drew close, they were cosily settled in the bothy again for another night and Chris said to Harry " The only person who could possibly turn up now would be a cyclist".

No sooner had he said it, in walked Tamy - full name Tamara Covacevich Stipicich who was from South Magallames in Chile. Her only comment was "oh are we sharing?" They got on so well and spent the evening sharing stories. . Tamy was 27, originally from Patagonia in Chile and had covered a lot of the world in the last few years. She was currently working in London and had taken time off to travel to the islands. They had a great evening sharing stories and experiences. Tamy was such an interesting and widely travelled person for someone so young.

The highlight of the evening though was when Chris introduced Tamy to Marmite. She absolutely loved it and couldn't believe the many uses, especially when Chris made a hot drink out of it. She took loads of photos of the lads and the Marmite. Well, you either love it or hate it don't you? She was lovely company.

The lads knew they had to be up early the next morning because the bus was at 7:15 am so they explained to Tamy that they needed to get their head down. What an amazing young woman she was. Her reaction when she arrived could have been "what the heck are you doing here?' as she had probably booked it for that evening but instead she welcomed the company and they got on really well. Tamy said that she would contact Leo on Messenger when she got back and stay in touch with the lads for when they published the tale of their travels and with that they all retired for the night. Harry wrote in his diary before going into the land of Nod, " The visit to Eagles Nest has been amazing would not have missed this for the world. Chris has been in his element. It's 9pm and going to bed. Good night all "

Photo – Tamy and the lads in the bothy sharing Marmite

It had been worth the wait and the effort and the distance travelled. Many things in life don't quite live up to the hype and the promise but the bothy at Mangersta had done that and more.

Eagles Nest had delivered the experience that the lads expected and although not an awful lot written in the diary it was because the lads simply soaked it all up and enjoyed their time just being in the place.

Harry's paella had gone down a bomb and Marmite had just boosted sales in South America if Tamy's reaction was anything to go by.

HEBRIDEAN HOSPITALITY

Day 17 – Eagles Nest to Stornaway – Monday 23rd of May

They woke around 4.00am. Rations were now low having spent a further night in the bothy. They had one shortbread finger biscuit between them and a coffee. Now that doesn't sound a lot but if you could just listen to Chris talking about that one biscuit, you would think it was the most satisfying meal in the world. Chris's exact words? " It wasn't a question of - That'll have to do - It was a question of - Mmmmmm we have a biscuit – bloody luxury!"

Photo – The view outside the bothy.

They packed the rucksacks and left about 6:15am saying their goodbyes to Tamy. They walked over the cliffs and fields to the house. Got rid of their rubbish as instructed and left a £30 donation in a box left there for that purpose.

The bus came at 7:15am dead on and off they went. They travelled for a while on the bus to a house in the middle of nowhere. A boy came out dressed for school and then the bus travelled back to where it had picked the lads up.

It carried on going to other villages picking up people and around 8:10am they came to a bus stop layby where they all transferred to a larger coach for Stornoway.

The locals were amazing. It was all a story of co-operation and co-ordination. They handled their remoteness so efficiently and reminded the lads of the community spirit that used to exist all over the UK at one point but was now so rare, it was really noticeable.

After dropping all the children at their school, along with other bus loads arriving at the same time, the bus arrived in Stornoway about 8:50 am and the duo went straight to the Co-op and bought food and drink. They had to wait though until 10.00am before they could pay for beer (some rules don't change) so they went and had a coffee and a pastry.

When they got back to camp they went to see Dianne and booked four more nights in their tents and a final night in a pod so they could get organised for the ferry to Tarbert on Saturday morning.

In the afternoon they walked back into Stornoway to an ATM to get more money to pay Dianne and yes you guessed it, another pint in McNeil's Bar and headed for the Crown at 3pm, Debbie and her niece came in and wanted to know all about how they had got on at Eagle's Nest. She had told her mother-in-law all about them and was following their story on Facebook.

Harry took a photo of them and then the lads left and went for the bus at 5:50 pm. The next bus was in so they jumped on that and was at the bottom of the lane for 6.00pm.

They walked to the tents and then Harry started cooking. Chris opened a beer and Harry went to Chris's tent about an hour later and delivered his evening meal to him – cooked and diced chicken and mushrooms, spinach, broccoli, peaches and spicy rice. Harry said "It was bloody good, even though I cooked it myself"

Harry chatted to Ian and Callum, a father and son from Peterburgh. Callum got onto Chris's Facebook page as they were very interested in what the lads were doing. Harry got a photo with them, had his tea and washed up and then wrote in his diary.

End of another super day – it's now 10pm good night all.

Day 18 – Stornaway to A&E - Tuesday, 24th of May

Harry woke at 5 am and immediately went and had a shave and shower as the pair of them literally hadn't washed for three days. The shower felt so good. The clothes he took off all walked into a wash bag themselves with the underpants humming a tune!!

He went to the kitchen and started breakfast. Two lots of sausages, square sausages, black pudding and two eggs. The cramp in Harry's right leg had returned and it was now getting a little worrying. He knew he would have to have it checked before they did anything else. When they were both ready, they walked to the Stornoway hospital just down the road. When they arrived, the receptionist, Donna, asked if they had phoned.

Harry explained that they were walkers doing the Hebridean way and the lady gave him forms to fill-in. They then waited about two hours and the nurse took them in and examined Harry, took his temperature, blood pressure and blood samples.

A doctor came in and checked him over and said she was going to get Harry an ultrasound scan to check for DVT (Deep Vein Thrombosis). Luckily, all came back clear. The nurse then dressed Harry's blisters and gave him extra medical pads to put on later himself.

Donna in reception then took them both to a private room and said "wait here while I get you both coffee and toast". How good was that? They don't do that at North Manchester A&E! There's something else they don't do too. Donna came back later and had brought the lads Lasagna and chips for their tea for when they get back to camp. Amazing!

The doctor had gone through the results of all the tests with Harry and said to him that there was no real damage but he was simply carrying too much weight with his rucksack.

Chris left Harry resting and walked into Stornoway for something for tea, some beers and also got some stuff for breakfast. They gave Harry a pair of crutches to take the weight off his right leg and Harry had told them that they would drop them off on Friday before they left. Donna said "leave them with Diane at the camp she's a friend of mine she will give them to me".

HEBRIDEAN HOSPITALITY

When they arrived back at camp Diane came over to see how Harry was. They chatted and Harry asked her if she had an OXO cubes. "No" she said "but I have Bisto granules" She came back with them and said she had also baked a ginger cake and gave them four huge thick slices. For the umpteenth time the lads both looked at each other as if to say "Is this place heaven or not?"

They had their tea and Leo rang them to see how things were and the lads spoke to him for a while, especially about the amazing people who had been helping them. After a while both lads got into their wind down routine involving a couple of beers and while Chris listened to music in his tent, Harry washed up and retired to his tent and updated his diary at just 8.10pm.

Photo: **A&E Stornaway – If Carlsberg did hospitals…..**

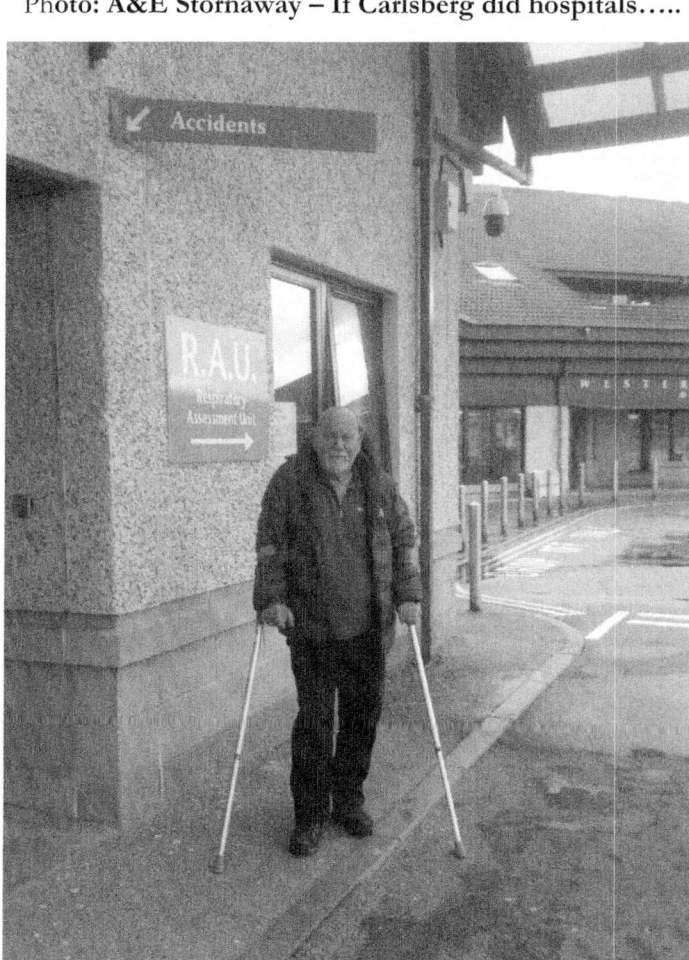

Day 19 – Stornaway - Wednesday, 25th of May

Harry woke at 6.00am and his legs were beginning to feel better already. He would persist with the crutches for a while as they were clearly helping him by keeping the weight off his right leg.

Shower, shave and breakfast of Shreddies and coffee. Sounds a little healthier approach to breakfast but then he finished it off with a piece of Dianne's ginger cake. "Delicious". Said Harry.

Chris of course was already showered and shaved and had been up with the birds at around 5.00am. They got the 9:30am bus to Stornoway, shopped in Tesco and then to the Smokery to get more kippers.

They then headed over to the Tourist Information centre to see Karen. They had a laugh about how things had turned out and also did a mock video with the weather report for the BBC from Stornoway presented by Harry Bentley, Chris Duoba, Karen and guest star young Cory with the map in the background.

Photo: Karen and Cory putting together their weather report

They did try and send the video on to Leo but with no joy .Harry was having a little problem with storing photos and videos on his phone. They headed into a photo shop in Stornaway to try and fix this.

The guy at the shop unlocked 147 pictures and printed them all for Harry for £29.50 and then cleared the photos off his phone to free up some memory, including all of his Whatsapp photos.

Then it was a few pints of Guinness in The Crown and headed for the 3:40pm bus to Laxdale camp. Harry cooked burgers and black pudding topped with melted cheese (so bad for you but so good) and delivered Mr Duoba's to his tent. It was a Hebridean Deliveroo.

Couple of beers and that's Chris out for the count. Harry had his and read the local newspaper, washed up and that's him gone for the night too.

Harry wrote in the diary that the weather forecast for the next day or so was looking grim but it was about resting his leg for two more days and then leaving for Tarbert.

Photo – On the road to Laxdale Campsite

HEBRIDEAN HOSPITALITY

Day 20 – Stornaway - Thursday, the 26th of May

Harry woke at about 7:30 which seemed like a lie in now for him. Chris was outside the kitchen drinking coffee when Harry opened his tent flap. They had kippers and poached eggs for breakfast. 'This is amazing' said Chris.

Harry washed up and had a quick chat with Dianne and then the lads got the bus to Stornoway. Their routine for this last few days was not broken so why fix it. Tesco for food and beer and the smokehouse for kippers for Friday.

They then headed for the cultural centre to book tickets to see a film that had been made locally called 'Road House' which Harry says is about a local girl. Leo wrongly thought that Road House was a film with Patrick Swayze. It didn't really matter which film it was because it was fully booked up with a waiting list for a 2 o'clock matinee. They were gutted.

They walked around the docks and marina and were amazed at some of the boats. They grabbed some cash from the ATM and then headed for the doctor's surgery for some medicine – well, it wasn't actually the doctors, it was the Crown Inn and it was three pints of medicine.

They walked back later along the docks as Harry had asked a man cleaning the fish fridge van about some scallops' shells. He directed them to a shop further along the quay. Harry asked a young woman cleaning baskets with a pressure washer where they could find the shells and she said "we have some in the back". Harry asked "do you have two dozen?" and she gave them 20. 'How much do I owe you" said Harry. she just said "you can have them" " Thank you very much" said Harry who would use them at home for presentation of food. They were chuffed to bits and went for the bus back.

They got off the bus at Laxdale lane and was in camp for about 4.15pm. They sat and had a beer and then started tea which tonight was Meatballs, tomato and mascarpone sauce, spinach and noodles and of course a couple more beers. Fantastic!. Chris took his food and his beers to his tent and said good night.

Harry had a chat with two people, Paul and Lindsay from Stirling before retiring and he wrote his diary in the kitchen while they cooked their tea. "What lovely people" He added "Just finishing my beer and diary 8:05 pm - Good night"

Day 21 – Stornaway - Friday, the 27th of May

Harry woke about 5:30 am. Chris was already showered and having a coffee. Harry's Leg was still hurting but a little less. The lads enjoyed their Kippers for brekkie. "delicious" they both said.

Dianne came to see them as they had booked a pod for their last night tonight and she said she was going to check on the "Wigwam". People had left early so she cleaned it and said they could move. Chris emptied the tents into the Wigwam and they organised all the stuff that needed to dry and washed up.

Photo: Dianne at Laxdale – An angel – so kind and helpful

The lads then went into their new daily routine of heading into Stornoway to shop. They got food for a Friday night meal, which was to be a paella but with pepperoni mushrooms spinach broccoli runner beans fiery rice and prawns.

They purchased two boxes of chocolates for the girls at the hospital and a box for Diane at the campsite and went to The Crown for their usual 3 pints and to say their goodbyes . Chris particularly loved The Crown Inn because there was no loud music and everyone was so civilised. It meant so much to

HEBRIDEAN HOSPITALITY

him to be able to relax and meet people without the din that sometimes exists in pubs and distracts him ever since his accident over 40 years ago.

They went for the early bus to hospital and dropped off chocolates (and crutches) and said their thanks and goodbyes. They hobbled back to the campsite and were having a beer sat outside the office when Diane came and said " Boys I've baked you a cake for your last night – Enjoy". They were overwhelmed. These people were just amazing. They were tourists at the end of the day but they had been treated like relatives and friends. They thanked her profusely.

The lads had their last night meal and it was delicious washed down with a couple of beers. It was a warm night and Chris put his headphones on and was away with the fairies. Harry also had a great sleep and made a compromise of rather than hobbling to the loo in the middle of the night, he found his tin mug doubled really well as a night time piss pot and washed out thoroughly for his morning coffee - Do Not Try This At Home!! They were both tucked up in their tents by 8pm and Harry forced down a slice of Diane's cake to finish off the evening and empty the last bit of his tea in his mug ready for the night. Stornaway had been such a great base for the lads and the people there were amazing.

Photo – Stornaway harbour and the aptly named boat 'Gratitude'

HEBRIDEAN HOSPITALITY

Day 22 - Stornaway to Skye - Saturday 28th of May

Harry woke up about 5:30 am. Chris was up having a coffee. Harry went with stuff to the kitchen then went for a shave and shower and felt great after. Breakfast was mushrooms on a crusty roll top with a fried egg and a coffee.

Dianne and others not there yet and the lads had to leave. So, they left the chocolates and a photo of the three of them in the wigwam They walked to the bus stop and got the bus to Stornaway to the bus station. Their bus came in 8:45 am and they asked the driver if they could leave their rucksacks on the bus. The driver told them to put them in the boot and hand luggage in the bus and be back for 9.45am.

They went to the Crown Inn for coffee and took a photo of the bar. They went for the bus and the driver let them on for £4.88 for 37 miles. The driver also loaded fish, greengrocery and parcels for delivery on the way to Tarbert.

They arrived at 10:45am and went to the waiting room, paid a visit and then walked down the hill to the Hebridean hotel. They had one pint of Guinness and spoke to Tommy who served them during the weekend they spent in Tarbert. They took a photo of the staff, who were all great people and then went for the ferry at 12 noon crossing from Tarbert to Uig on Skye.

They arrived in Uig about 1pm. On the corner at the terminal was a bus heading all the way to Glasgow. The lads got on for as far as Portree heading south down Skye. - £11.20 for two singles for the 16-mile journey. Not exactly Hebridean prices.

The lads arrived in Portree about 2:30pm and went straight to the tourist information office to try and locate a camp site. They met a lady called Wendy and she remembered a conversation with Harry months previously. There were no campsites in Portree and the B&Bs were all full. Wendy and Stephen, who worked there, phoned all over for them and then they struck gold. They found them a plot at a Campsite at Kinloch overlooking the village of Dunvegan with spectacular views across the loch up into the mountains. It was 23 miles west of where they were but they were glad to find somewhere.

They got a bus over and set up their tents for the night and went into the village. They ended up with fish and chips at a place called the Old School

House and had to eat outside costing £25. They had a wander down the road and The Atholl Hotel B&B which was open to non-residents. Chris really enjoyed it because it was quiet. They had three bottles of Skye black which is a bit like Guinness but lighter. They booked a table to eat there for Sunday evening about 5 pm. They finished their drinks and walked back to campsite and were in bed for 9pm.

Harry made his diary entry and reflected on the change of feeling to the trip. He thought 'it's not the Hebrides - Skye is a great place but just too commercialised for them both at this point in their trip"

Photo: Information required at Portree

HEBRIDEAN HOSPITALITY

Day 23 – Dunvegan, Skye - Sunday, the 29th of May

Harry woke about 6:30 am and went for a shower and shave and when he got back Chris had brewed up. They sat on the grass and ate some of Diane's cake. There are of course lots of things to see and do on Sky and some very popular places like the "Fairypools and Waterfalls" which involves a stunning walking route with some amazingly beautiful scenery but Chris and Harry were still not feeling it and missed the chilled atmosphere of the Hebridean islands.

Later, they walked into Dunvegan and went to a place called Misty's for a coffee and Chris said, "I don't like it here on Skye. The place itself is absolutely beautiful but there are too many tourists" Harry admitted he'd had the same thoughts. So, they decided that on Monday they would travel to Portree and try and get a bus to Fort William. They would then have a choice of staying over at Fort William or catch a train to Glasgow then home.

It felt like an anti-climax to the trip but it also felt time to go home. If they had landed on Skye first and then gone to the Outer Hebrides this would have had a very different effect on the lads but they hadn't and now they were not enjoying the bustle of lots of tourists. Of course, there are people who like just the opposite so it is so important that you know what you want from visiting the islands before you travel and plan things accordingly. Later that day they made their way to The Atholl Hotel and had a couple of drinks then sat down to eat. The food was to die for. Harry had duck comfit with potatoes and veg and gravy. Chris had hot salmon salad to start followed by chicken enchiladas in a rich tomato sauce with burritos. Harry finished with apple crumble with raisins and cinnamon. Wow, if this was to be the last night, what a great meal. Both of them were content that they may return home the next day and just chilled out with their last two pints of Skye Black.

They ended what was a great evening chatting to people from Germany and Oregon in America and not forgetting the staff at The Atholl Hotel who were first class; Jeni who owns it, Andrew her son who waits on, and Rachel and Sarah who the lads met the night before, had all been amazing hosts and Harry and Chris wished them well with their business for the future.

Day 24 – Skye to Manchester - Monday, the 30th May

The lads woke at 5:30 am, had a wash and then jointly packed everything to ensure that everything was in. At 7.00am they were ready to walk to the bus stop and arrived at 7:30 am.

The bus came at 8:05 am to Portree and was £11.80. They arrived in Portree about 8:45 am and had to wait for the bakery and tea shop to open but it was well worth the wait.

The lads had amazing crispy bacon rolls and coffee. They were so good that Harry ordered another one. – just a job. They managed to get on the Glasgow bus without booking. The single trip was £100 for the two of them. The bus left at 10:30am and arrived for a stop off in Fort William at 1:50 pm. The lads ran to a Morrisons quickly and grabbed some beers and water then jumped back on the bus. They'd lost their seats but made do with two more.

They were just glad to be on the way to Glasgow. An old couple got on and could not find two seats near each other so Harry jumped up and said to a young girl "your bag on the seat doesn't have a ticket does it? Well move it and let this gentleman sit down". She moved it and he sat down with his wife. Harry leaned over and said to the woman, "young people today just don't have manners" She smiled. This was a million miles away from the islands and the kind manner of everybody of every age.

They got to Glasgow at 5:45 pm. It had been a long day but there was still another leg to go. They walked over to Glasgow Central for the 18.20 p.m. Euston train which they then had to get off at Preston. From there, they phoned Leo who arranged to pick the lads up at Piccadilly station in Manchester.

Leo was there to greet them and the car on the way back home from the station was full of stories of the islands and the fantastic people they had met but Leo could also see the lads looking out of the windows at the hordes of people around the busy station and Manchester city centre.

After just a few weeks away on the Islands, it would take them both a little time to acclimatise back to city life but they wouldn't swap the trip for anything.

Photo – Back To The Future

The lads wanted to end the trip by sending the following message to the people who had helped them along the way

Message From Harry & Chris

"The Outer Hebrides is an amazing place to visit. The people there are even more amazing. Everywhere else looks highly commercialised in comparison, even the Isle of Skye. We will definitely be returning there one day. We would recommend it to anyone. Thanks so much to everyone over there for your kindness and the wonderful welcoming feeling you gave us everywhere we went. You are just the kindest people and we will never forget your wonderful......

Hebridean Hospitality.

Visit You Tube at https://youtu.be/yzlNCKgzkng

Photo: Harry 'The best bacon butty ever – found in Portree'

HEBRIDEAN HOSPITALITY

Photo: Last night at Laxdale in a 'pod'

Photo: Essential Equipment – Designer Beer Carrier

Photo: Chris leaves his book for some easy reading in the bothy

Photo: Laxdale Camp Site in summary

Photo: The mobile Fast-Food Van at Tarbert

Photo: Harry's tent from Willie's house

Photo: Harris to Lewis on the bus

Photo: The marker at the end of the Hebridean Way

Photo: The only lighthouse in the UK not to be painted

HEBRIDEAN HOSPITALITY

Photo: The queue at A&E

Photo: We knew Willie for 48 hrs but it felt like we'd known him years

Photo: Camp set up at Loch Seaforth

Photo: Alan Shearer is out for the season

HEBRIDEAN HOSPITALITY

Photo: Hurry up Harry it's freezing

Photo: Mangersta, Tamy's bike (centre) parked for Eagles Nest

Photo: Lews Castle

Photo: It doesn't get any more Hebridean than this

HEBRIDEAN HOSPITALITY

Photo: Harry soaks up the sun

Photo: Captain Chris arriving for his shift

Photo: Chris, harry and Eugene at The Isle of Barra Beach Hotel

HEBRIDEAN HOSPITALITY

Photo: Information Centre, Cromwell Street, Stornaway, Isle of Lewis

Telephone Number: 01851 703088

Photo: Information Centre, Bayfield Road, Portree, Isle of Skye

Telephone Number: 01478 612992

HEBRIDEAN HOSPITALITY

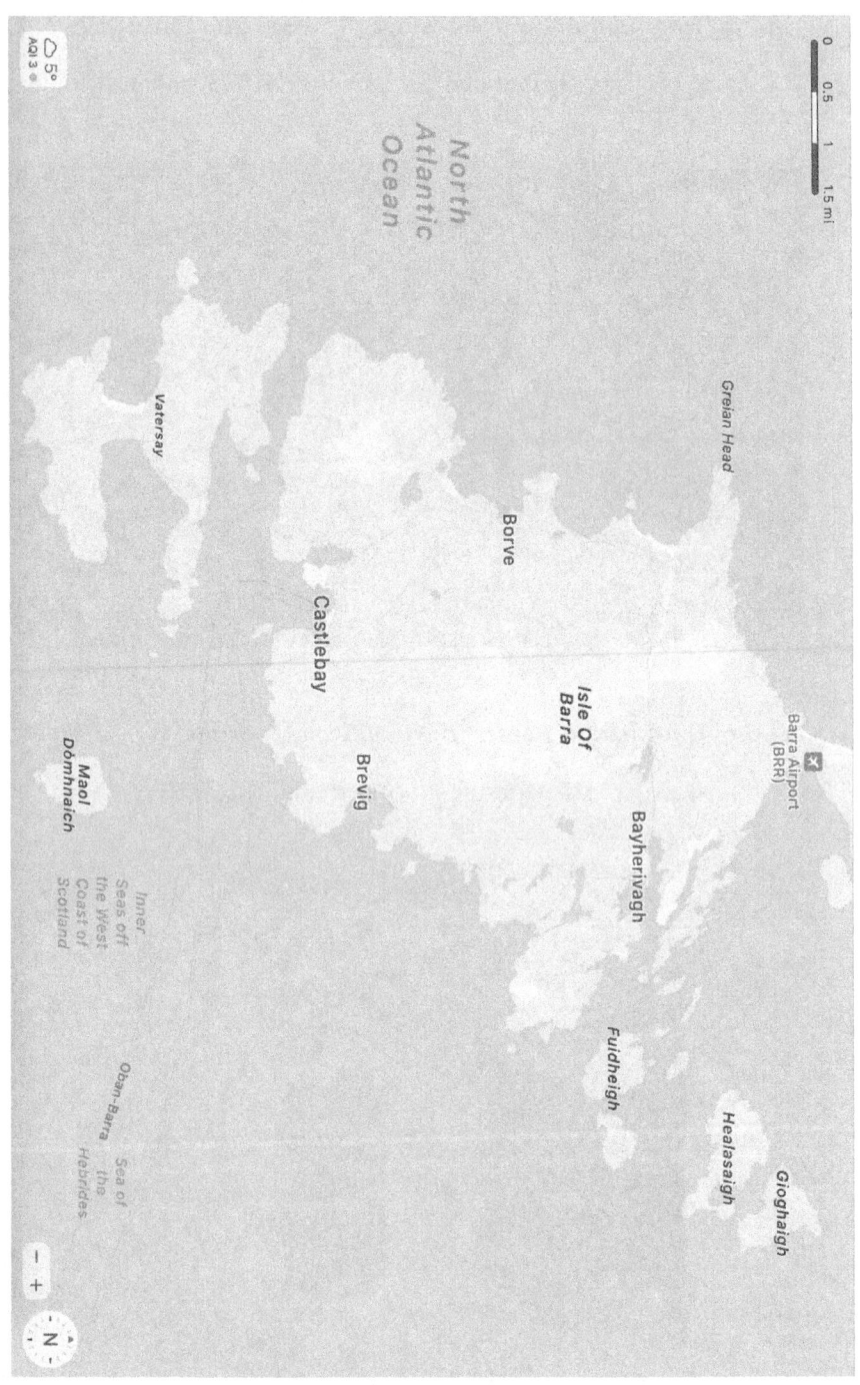

HEBRIDEAN HOSPITALITY

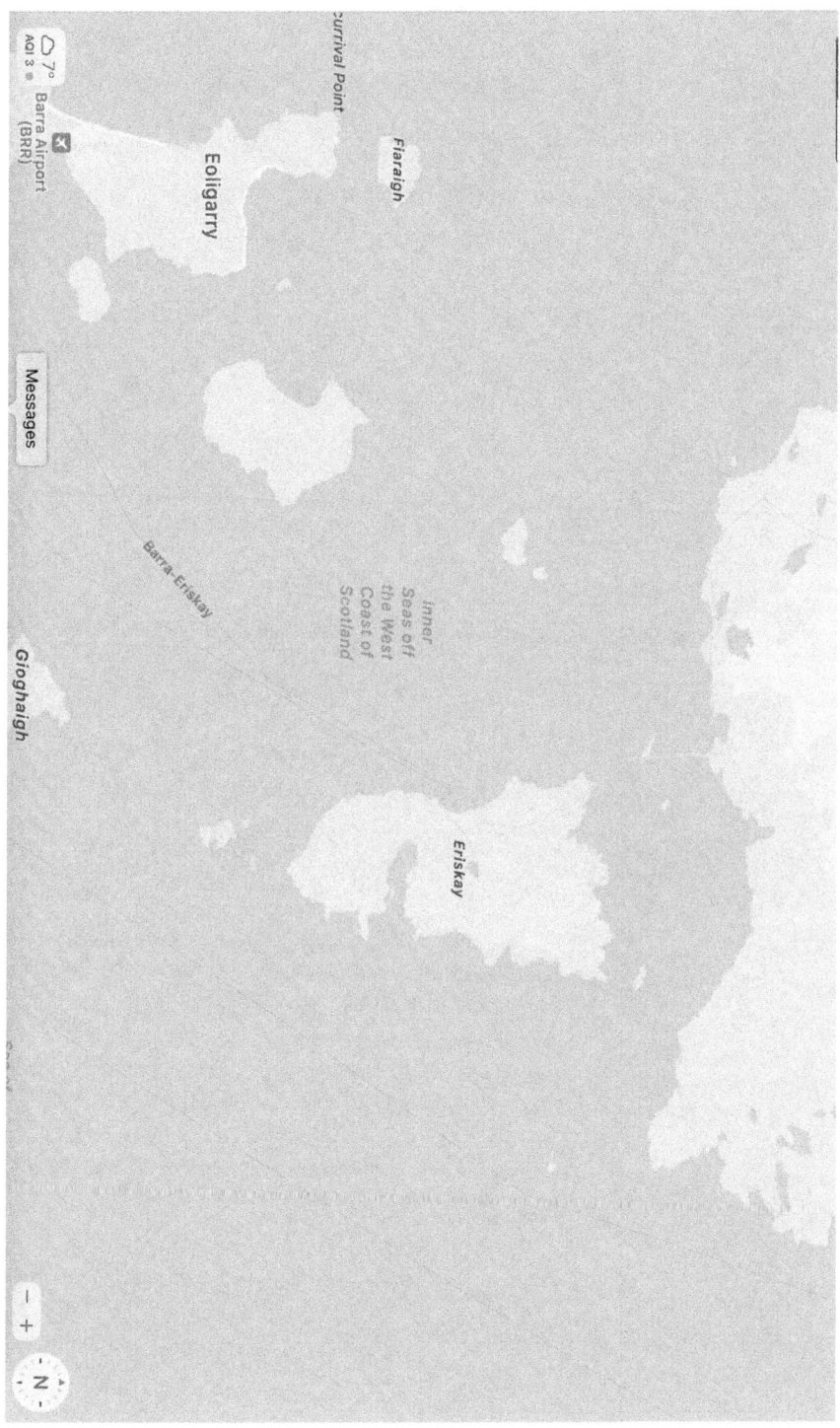

HEBRIDEAN HOSPITALITY

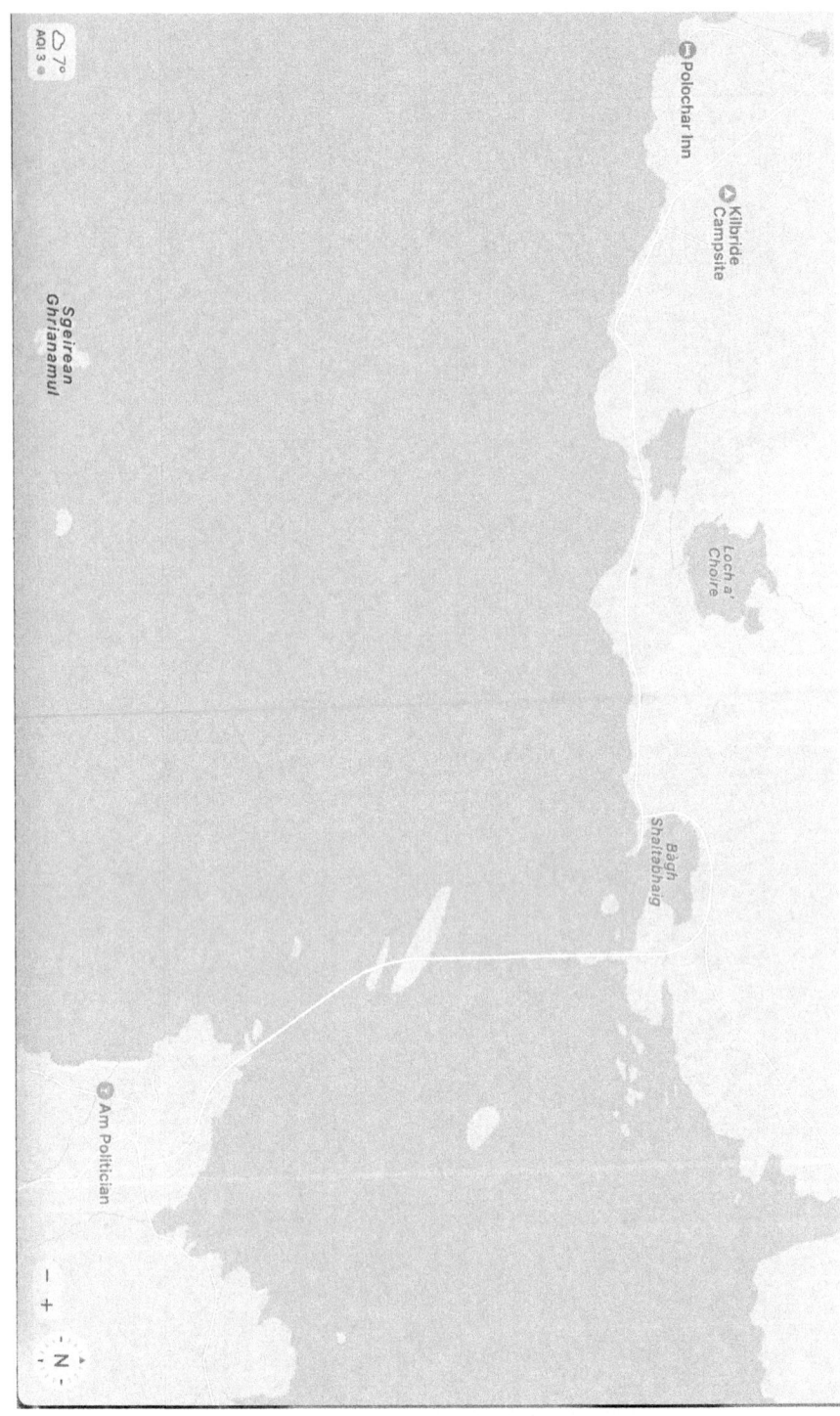

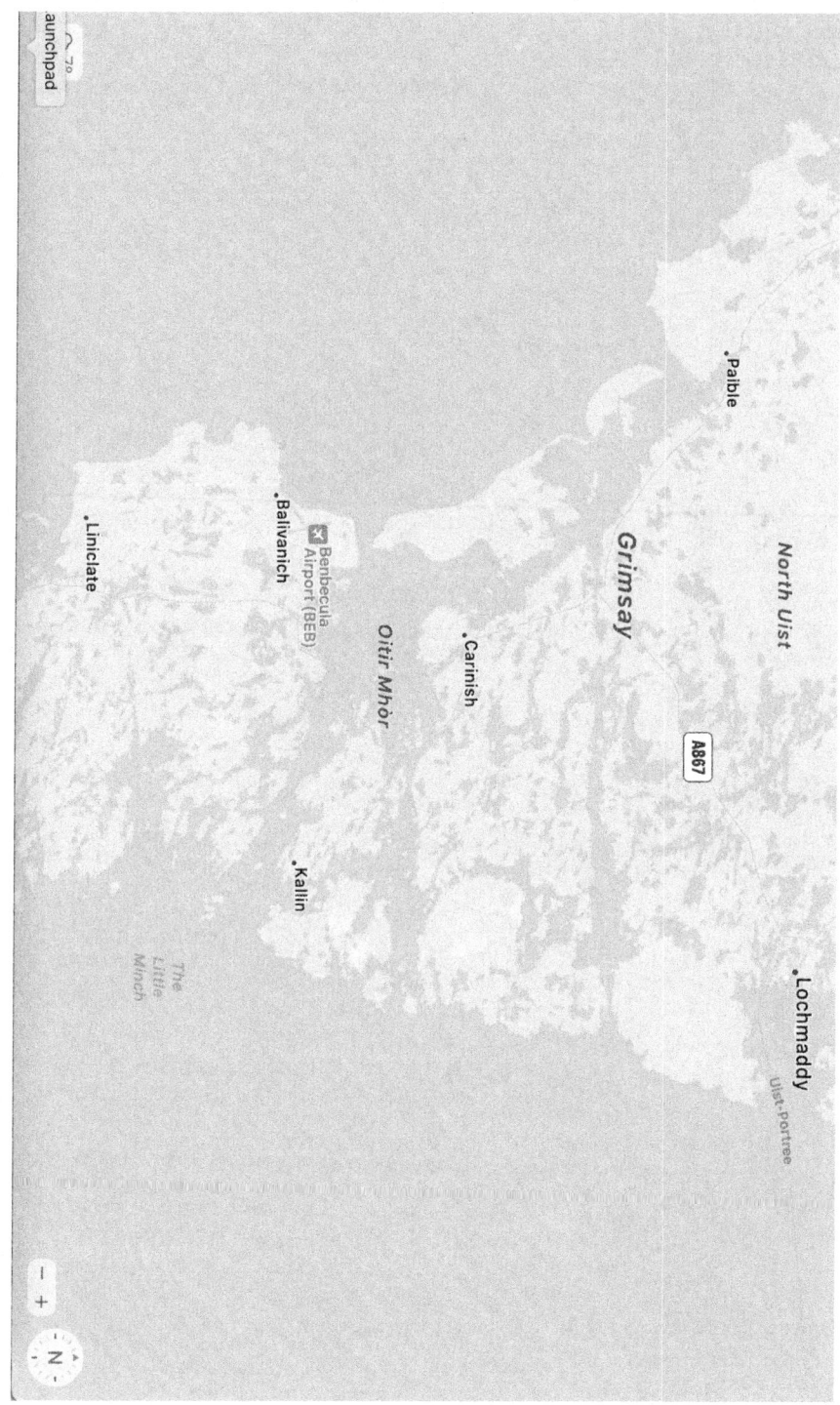

HEBRIDEAN HOSPITALITY

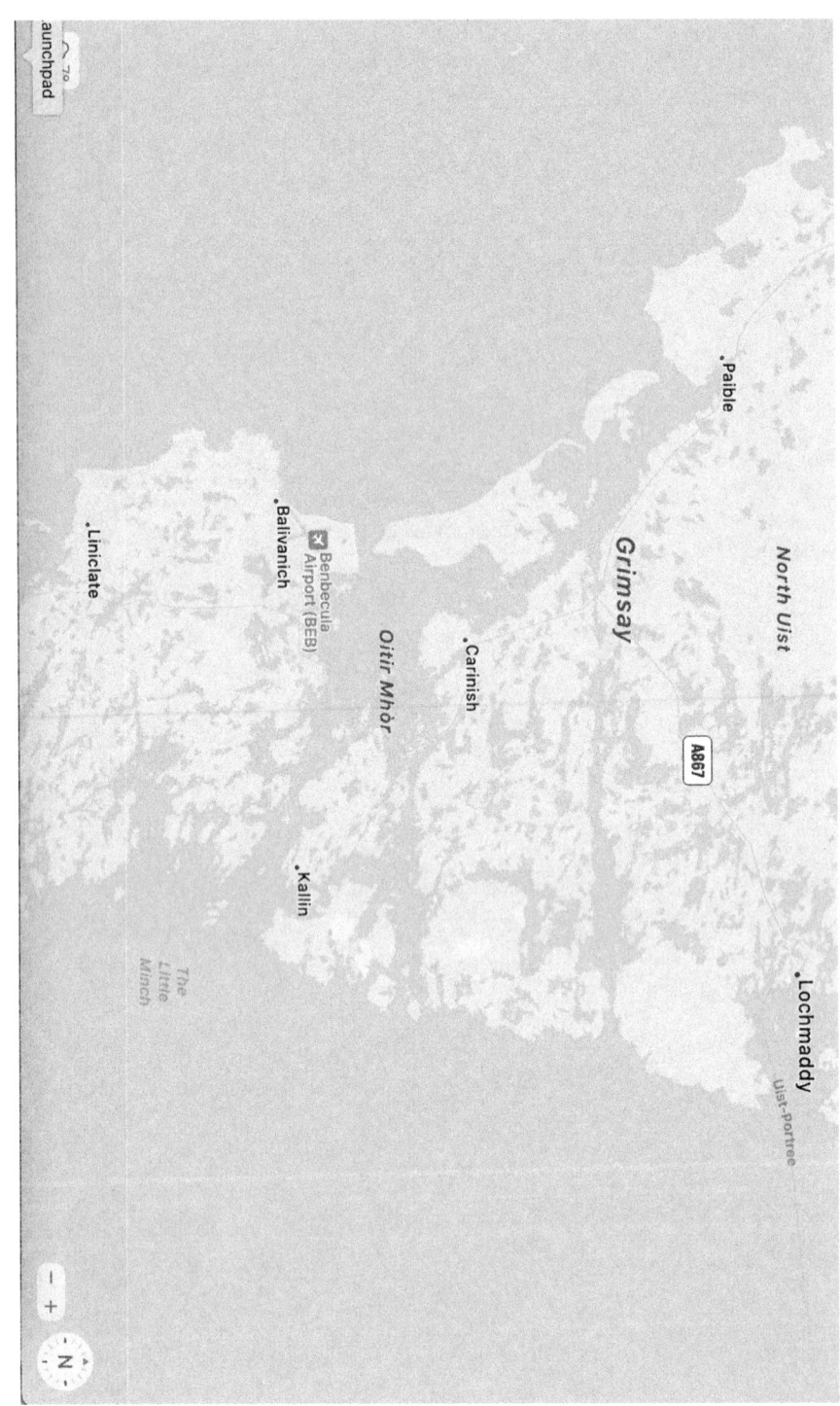

HEBRIDEAN HOSPITALITY

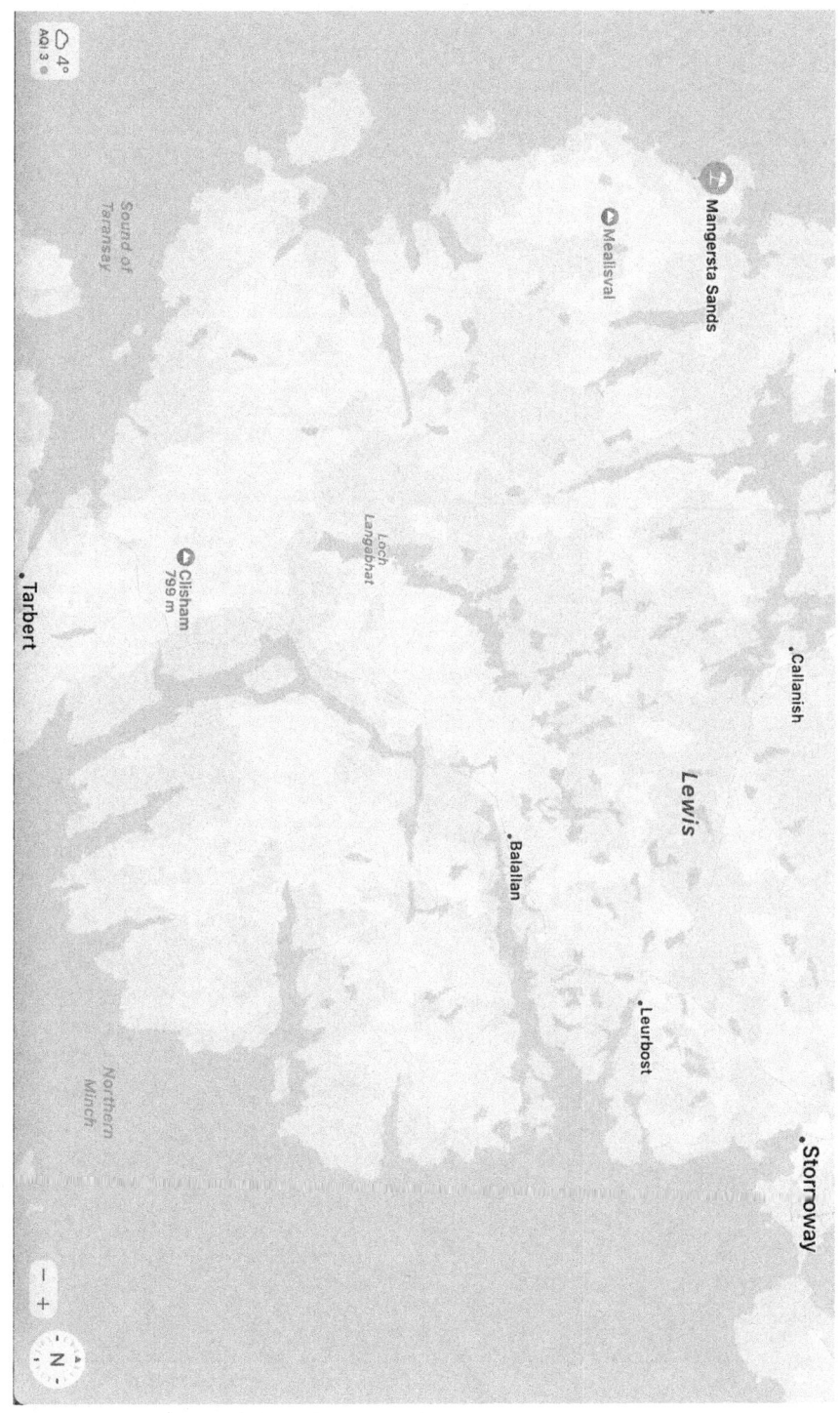

HEBRIDEAN HOSPITALITY

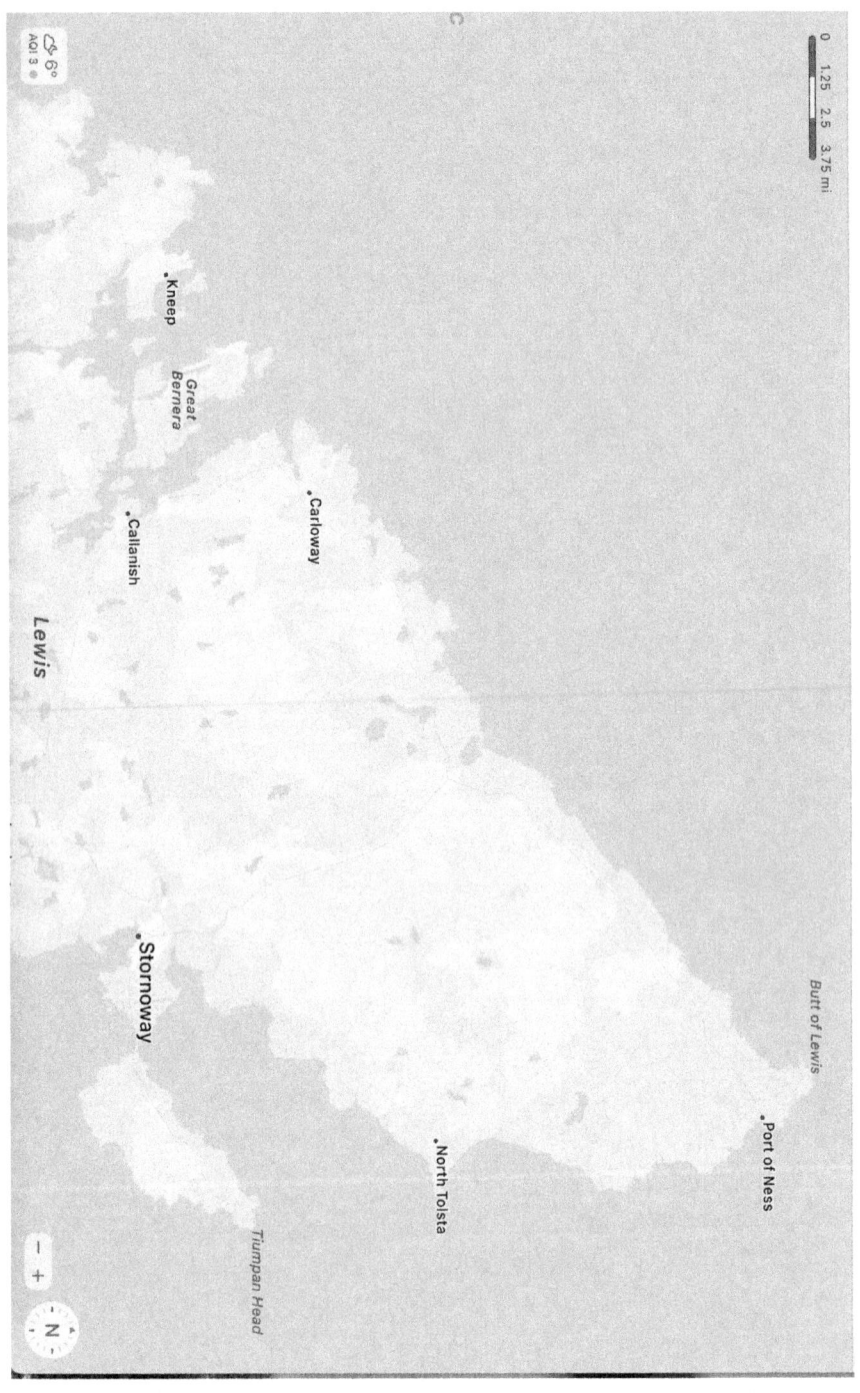

Thanks to anyone purchasing this booklet and being at all interested in the adventures of two guys who just treat age as a number and every day as a possible adventure.

HEBRIDEAN HOSPITALITY

Chris's amazing Life Story available on Amazon

ACKNOWLEDGEMENTS

Chris and Harry would like to personally thank the following for making their visit to the islands so memorable with their kindness and hospitality. They couldn't possibly thank them enough. In no particular order, these amazing people and businesses are:

- **Corran House Guest House & Hostel, Oban**
- The **Isle of Barra Beach Hotel,** Isle of Barra
- The wonderful staff at the **AM Politician pub, Eriskay, South Uist** for their hospitality.
- **Willie Irvine** A true gentleman and a scholar.
- The many thoughtful **coach drivers of the Western Isles** & particularly the Driver who stopped on the wrong side of the road to help us near Lochmaddy, **you are a gentleman sir.**
- **The Ferry Staff at Leverburgh,** Isle of Harris especially those who set the automatic door to lock us in from 7pm on 12th May until 7am on 13th May. Best night in a hotel ever.
- **Mr Morrison (Grocer shop / Tarbert)** for the smashing B&B.
- The staff at **The Hebridean Hotel bar**
- The staff at **Charlie's Food Wagon** on Main Street (Tarbert)
- A huge thank you goes to **Wendy and Steven** at the **Tourist Info (Portree)** and **Karen & Corrie** at the **Tourist Info Stornaway,** who made our trip so special with their guidance.
- Big thanks go to **Diane** at **Laxdale Holiday Park & Campsite** who not only looked after us but even baked us two cakes while we were there. The campsite is five-star in every way
- **The Staff at the Crown Inn in Stornoway** where we enjoyed many afternoons.
- A huge thank you to **the Staff at The Western Isles hospital** who looked after Harry and particularly **Donna** who went the extra mile for us and made sure we were fed and watered.

Last but certainly not least a big thank you to **Ann** at the **bus station Information Centre at Stornoway** who spoke with the lads on almost a daily basis.

HEBRIDEAN HOSPITALITY

For anybody interested in what constitutes a 30Kg comprehensive rucksack for a trip like the one tackled by Chris and Harry, this is roughly what would make wild camping a little easier. In no particular order, but with the advice that the best quality you can buy, then you do get what you pay for, especially with outdoor equipment and clothing, this is what constituted Chris's Rucksack and contents:

1 Rucksack (Chris used 'Osprey')	1 pair sandals for bath / shower / sea / swimming	Sun Cream (suitable to user)
I Angus Wall Tiger Tent	1 Swiss Knife (good quality one)	Soap
1 Space Blanket		Toothpaste
1 Thermal Mat	1 roll of Masking Tape	Blister treatment Packs
1 Sleeping Bag	Length of Rope	Insect Repellant
1 inflatable pillow	1 pack Spare Laces	Toilet Paper
1 Inflatable Mattress	I Pack Flat sponge wipes	Walking Poles (without the bus attached!!!)
1 Solar Panel Charger for Phone – decent quality.	Jet Boil and Gas	Warm Hat
1 Mobile phone with full access where a signal	Spare Food	Gloves
1 set of Waterproofs (invest in decent standard like 'Paramo')	Marmite	Compass
	Electrolyte tablets	
	Refillable bottle for water & 'Camelbak'	Head Torch
Several pieces of spare clothing in dry bag		Snood
	Gas lighter (& Battery) or fuel version	Poncho
1 Micro Towel	Medical & Washing Kit (see below)	Paper / Pencil /sharpener
Whistle		Frying Pan
Army Mess Tins	Hand Warmers	Spare Batteries

Printed in Great Britain
by Amazon